Sing

Stop

identify — main point

never mind the details

get the gist

To Overcome Laziness — Compelling Vision

1. What am I trying to avoid?
2. What is the best possible outcome? What will I gain
3. What is the <u>next</u> step? Take it
4. Repeat

# The Pleasure of His Company

## ROGER C. PALMS

Tyndale House Publishers, Inc.
Wheaton, Illinois

Second printing, June 1983
Library of Congress Catalog Card Number 82-60246
ISBN 0-8423-4847-6
Printed in the United States of America

*To Andrea*

*who encourages me*

# CONTENTS

# ACKNOWLEDGMENTS

The author wishes to acknowledge the following publications and publishers for material quoted in this book:

*Blood Brothers in Christ* by Malcolm Smith, copyright 1975. Permission granted by Malcolm Smith Ministries, Washingtonville, NY 10992.

*Calvin: Institutes of the Christian Religion,* edited by John T. McNeill, translated by Ford Lewis Battles (Volume XX: The Library of Christian Classics). Copyright © MCMLX W. L. Jenkins. Used by permission of The Westminster Press.

*Celebration of Discipline: The Path to Spiritual Growth* by Richard J. Foster. San Francisco: Harper & Row, Publishers, 1978. Used by permission.

*The Cost of Discipleship,* Second Edn., by Dietrich Bonhoeffer (© SCM Press Ltd., 1959). Used by permission.

*Discipleship* by A. H. McNeile. Copyright 1917 by The Society for Promoting Christian Knowledge. Used by permission.

*The Elements of the Spiritual Life* by F. P. Harton. Copyright 1950 by The Society for Promoting Christian Knowledge, London. Used by permission.

*Eternal Hope* by Emil Brunner, translated by Harold Knight. Published in the U.S.A. by The Westminster Press, 1954. Used by permission.

9

*Rediscovering the Church* by George Laird Hunt © 1953. By permission of New Century Publishers, Inc., Piscataway, NJ 08854.

*The Saints' Everlasting Rest* by Richard Baxter. London: The Epworth Press, 1962, used by permission.

*The Surrendered Life* by James H. McConkey. Copyright 1977 by Baker Book House and used by permission.

*A Testament of Devotion* by Thomas R. Kelly. Copyright 1941 by Harper & Row, Publishers, Inc. Used by permission.

*Upon a Penny Loaf* by Roger C. Palms. Published and copyright © 1978 by Bethany House Publishers, Minneapolis, MN 55438. Used by permission.

*The Way of Peace* by H. A. Ironsides, copyright 1940. Reprinted by permission of the American Tract Society, Garland, TX 75040.

*Western Asceticism,* edited by Owen Chadwick (Volume XII: The Library of Christian Classics). Published simultaneously by S.C.M. Press Ltd., London, and The Westminster Press, Philadelphia. First published in 1958. Used by permission.

# PREFACE

$W$hy struggle day in, day out, missing a life that was meant to be so special? If you have been grasping for meaning, yet wondering why you haven't found what deep down inside you really want—*then please stop!* It is time to turn around.

Commitment, discipline, understanding, holiness, and trust are the ingredients of a rewarding life based on the deepest of all relationships—your friendship with God. God wants you to have that. The only question is, do you want it too?

Come, discover this friendship, and enter into the pleasure of his company.

# ONE
# Sand Castles Don't Last

† *Every one that heareth these sayings of mine, and doeth them not, shall be likened unto a foolish man, which built his house upon the sand: and the rain descended, and the floods came, and the winds blew, and beat upon that house; and it fell: and great was the fall of it. And it came to pass, when Jesus had ended these sayings, the people were astonished* [Matthew 7:26–28, kjv].

One afternoon in Paris I tried to absorb with my senses the Cathedral of Notre Dame, that beautiful Gothic structure built in the Middle Ages. There was so much to enjoy aesthetically: the altar appointments, the smell of candles, the feel of old polished wood, the great rose windows, the awesome grandeur of the organ sounding through that massive building. . . . It could have been a memorable and serene experience. It turned out to be memorable, but it wasn't serene. In front of me, darting quickly here and there with cameras rapidly clicking, were dozens of tourists scurrying through the cathedral. They had only a few minutes before returning to their waiting tour buses for a fast drive to some other historic spot where they would click their cameras some more.

15

Pushing past other people, they raced first to one side, then to the other, frantically working their cameras. Then they were gone, only to be replaced—to my exasperation—by another busload of tourists all bent on doing the same thing.

I had made no other plans for that afternoon. Meditation in that historic place, quiet prayer, and the enjoyment of the beauty were what I had wanted. But I couldn't shut out the confusion around me.

Finally I left. On the way out I walked behind an American couple. The man had a checklist in his hand. As they stepped into the sunlight, the man asked his wife, "Was that the Cathedral of Notre Dame?" She answered that it was. With that confirmation, he took out his pencil, ticked off that item on his tour list, and they hurried away. They will probably tell their friends that they have seen Notre Dame; perhaps they'll show slides and rave about how much they enjoyed their visit. Unhappily, they didn't really see it at all.

Man seems desperate to experience, yet he really doesn't experience anything. He goes through the act of looking but rarely knows the joy of seeing.

It is as if all of us are on an ocean beach called Earth. We are frantic. We build castles—or at least we think we do. But what we are really doing is just throwing up sand piles as fast as we can before the next big wave comes in. And that wave is coming. We can't run from it; there's no escaping it. We will stay on the beach building our castles higher, bigger, more elaborate. We won't enjoy them. There will be no time for that. The wave is coming.

There have been other waves; tides have risen and ebbed. This is our time. Our little shovels flash in the sun as we dig in the midst of other frenzied diggers, each trying to heap more sand before the end. Never mind the next person's castle; never mind the next person at all. Just build. Dig, dig, dig. Keep an eye on the wave . . . a few more seconds. It's coming—grab one more bit of sand. . . .

Look at those fistfuls of sand. What is that sand that runs through fingers, that won't pack down, won't hold? *Things,* maybe; that's always the start of the grabbing. *Pleasure,* usually; that's the drive. Grabbing things and pleasures, tangible and sensual, is our attempt to get more of what has always given us security. But they don't any longer.

We know that our old systems are in crisis, and no one seems to have new or better answers. Each of us thinks, "I've got to look out for me and mine. And the only way I know is the familiar way. I've got to go for what has always worked. I'll reach for more of what I know."

The social confusion, the sex exploitation, the deterioration of family and home, and the end of cultural stability are all exploding around us. We do all we know to do. Afraid to be left behind, we grasp for even more. And the deterioration quickens.

Logic would tell us that if the end is coming, there is no need to grab for things and pleasures, because they're temporary. But we aren't logical. What we face is a deeper fear, a fear based on emptiness. And that hideous emptiness causes us to clutch to ourselves what has always given security and pleasure before.

So we are desperate and don't even know what we are desperate for. We are in a frightening world and do not understand it. We have lost our grip on soci-

17

ety, on culture, on family, on stable value systems, and with our fingernails torn, our fingertips bleeding, we feel it all slipping from our grasp. We *want*. We don't know what it is that we want, but we want something and we want it now. It is a hurting pressure, a feeling that, whatever that something is that we want, it is out of our grasp and we must grab whatever else is close—anything.

What is happening to us? We have done more than spawn a generation caught in the mindset of self. We have created a human religion that is insatiable in its thirst, with great yearnings, yet with no way to satisfy those yearnings. We are junkies overdosing on ourselves even though we know there isn't a high in it anymore. Nothing satisfies. So we try harder, push farther, and grasp for still more, for whatever might give some hope that our emptiness will be filled.

People have always built sand castles, and those castles have always crumbled. There have always been those who grabbed for things that break. But now it is like the beginning of the end, like the first moments of a stock market crash, and the scramble is on. And even as the social commentators begin to write about the cultural phenomena of these times, as psychologists give their explanations and theologians theirs, the frustration of wanting and not finding is already so much a part of the way people think that it is difficult for any to be objective in their analysis: these interpreters of us are on the beach too, grasping their own handfuls of sand.

The experts can't agree on the reasons for our sand-castle mentality, of course, but they usually agree on the data about it. For even before the early energy crises hit, before credit costs skyrocketed, before inflation and unemployment mounted, optional pleasures once called "extras" were gorged upon, and pleasure was what mattered. It was a beginning of something bigger, deeper.

At first, newspaper advertisements called it "the good life." We were told "to grab for," "you deserve," "like it, charge it." And in our "there-is-no-tomorrow" mentality, that is what we did. The results are easily traced now: consumption, depletion of natural resources, physical stress, emotional breakdown, family and marital discord, crime. And sadly, we pretended that we were happy—or soon would be. We pretended that we controlled our madness. We didn't; we don't.

Recently, in a test given by a popular magazine on people's "happiness quotient," it was shown that people have crossed the line from trying to make themselves happy to just plain racing to grab for anything that they don't now have. A few years ago *The New York Times* counted 3,000 diet books, 2,000 self-improvement books, at least 1,000 sex manuals on the market. Bookstore owners said that people were looking for answers. And when religious leaders started promoting self-help and self-transformation books, we knew that even Christians had crossed a line. Self-help was charted by publishers, simplified by writers, and swallowed up by readers. As Christians, we learned how we could lose weight, enjoy sex, be assertive, or negotiate so that anyone could be a winner. God in his wonder, majesty, and strength was to be *utilized:* to love him was self-loving as we "sensitized" ourselves to his wonder, majesty, and strength. We tried to have him shaped, packaged, wrapped, marketed, and consumed.

Pathetic? Yes, it is. And with the increase in what are sometimes little more than Christian roadshows, the availability of the media to them, and the willingness of churches to be booking agents for any new act that comes to town, more and more people started asking for the unusual and exciting rather than the Answer. We found people-exploiters to tell us that life should be a miracle every minute with a continuous feeling of ecstasy and joined the rest of the desperate people building their sand castles on the beach.

Like a dog chasing its own tail, we chase after what is always eluding us. What we want is always just out of reach, never quite within our grasp, yet always in sight—the back end of something going away which we must catch before it disappears.

John Bunyan, the seventeenth-century tinker-turned-preacher, described people like us as boys who chase butterflies:

> Behold how eager our little boy
> Is for this butterfly, as if all joy,
> All profits, honors, and lasting pleasures,
> Were wrapt up in her—or the richest treasures
> Found in her—
> When her all is lighter than a feather.
>
> He halloos, runs, and cries out, "Here, boys,
>   here."
> Nor doth he brambles or the nettles fear.
> He stumbles at the molehills; up he gets,
> And runs again, as one bereft of wits,
> While all his labor and this large outcry
> Is only for a silly butterfly.

*This little boy is much like those*
*Whose hearts are wholly at the world's dispose.*
*The butterfly does represent to me*
*The world's best things, at best but fading be.*
*All are but painted nothings and false joys,*
*Like this poor butterfly to these our boys.*
*His running through the nettles, thorns and briars*
*To gratify his boyish fond desires;*
*His tumbling over molehills to attain*
*His end, namely his butterfly to gain,*
*Plainly shows what hazards some men run*
*To get what will be lost as soon as won.*
*Men seem, in choice, than children far more wise*
*Because they run not after butterflies,*
*When yet, alas, for what are empty toys*
*They follow them, and act as beardless boys.*

It is a frantic chase when we run after butterflies as little boys do. We go first here, then there; we can't rest as long as we see anything that glitters in the sun. We dart along our zigzag courses, trying to catch that elusive pretty thing. But our chasing only tires us.

To one degree or another, the "hurry-up-and-grab, then-run-for-more" people are addicts, and these addicts seem to be everywhere, including the church. Chasing butterflies has become so commonplace that some have even stamped it "approved" by Jesus. He never did approve it. By the measure of Scripture, he never will.

Originally, the race was run toward happiness. Now the race goes on only for the sake of the race. We should have known that it would be that way because the obvious mark of a truly happy person is that he needs nothing more, and so many of us act as if we need more of everything. A happy person has mastered his conflicts, but this quest that was once a quest for happiness is now itself the cause of conflict. The happy life is a pleasant life, yet our lives are filled with neuroses.

There are no age limits to this sickness. We have taught our "religion" well. In a newspaper interview a. seventeen-year-old boy admitted: "I worry a lot. I'm running at a ninety-mile-an-hour pace. I feel like I've lived nineteen or twenty more years because of that feeling of 'I've got to get to work now.'" An eighteen-year-old high school boy said, "I want to be comfortable. I just want to be happy and have money to do the things I want to do." And several in a group said, "Give us comfort, and give us the money to buy it with."

One seventeen-year-old said that failure is not having a job that gets you enough money. Teens use money for clothes, food, entertainment, cars, and stereos, in that order. A high school English teacher commented that in eighteen years of teaching she has never seen students who are so materialistic. Then she added: "The whole nation is going that way." And as this grabbing occurs, teenagers scream at their parents, "You've used yours; you've taken the resources. We want ours too before it's all gone." The frenzy spreads.

The passion changes, or appears to, by the gyrations of the economy or the threats of war—and war itself. It changes by the influence of films, advertising, and books. And yet it doesn't really change; it continues to build with a collective madness.

We face the consequences now. What started with

the "me" decade is now part of the destruction of people labeled "snapping," a falling out of awareness. People are lost. Maybe they know it's happening; maybe they don't want to know it. A. H. McNeill, in his book *Discipleship,* tells us, "There are multitudes of people who seldom or never think. Their life is like the thinnest of rafts, floating upon an ocean of infinite mystery; and they hate to be asked to look over the edge. They are very busy decking out their raft with everything which can make it feel like a permanent home. . . . They never realize that they are on a raft and not a rock, until one day an illness or an accident or a war flicks them off into the ocean, where they have never learnt to swim."

Even the traditional obedience to societal structure or family, which might have taught us a larger view of ourselves, has disappeared. Any inner hint that true meaning might be found outside ourselves is dismissed or denied and leaves people sad, pathetic, anguished. There is no frame of reference or justification for our being, other than to take and use more. We have successfully eliminated all controls, and have shed ourselves of responsibilities.

This is man's religion. Even those who never quote the creed have come to live by it. For it isn't only the secular man who is caught; many who wear the label "Christian" have been snared too. Many who speak of being made alive by God really have no idea how satisfying that life in God can be. They're too busy looking elsewhere to find out. Like the characters in Russell Conwell's famous lecture "Acres of Diamonds," they're always looking over someone else's fence for the gems.

They have tried, along with everyone else, to make

some sense of their existence. They have looked for the action, gotten involved, given themselves to causes, traveled inward, entered analysis, meditated, tried health foods—anything that might give them what everyone else seems to be chasing. They have gone sermon-tasting and liturgy-hunting, seeking answers from pulpits and prayer groups like so many door-bangers on a pub crawl. They have joined Christian political groups, partied at Christian night spots, and hastened to seminars for the latest spiritual word from whoever is currently big on the Christian circuit. But all they have discovered is that none of us can get what he wants that way.

We are, as the rest of mankind is discovering, far more complex than we thought. We are more than a soul to be "sensitized," more than an ego to be stroked, more than a mind to be taught. We are wonderfully put together into a self, and with all of our searching we have not been able to make sense of it all. We still cry out for something.

Our needs become a search and our search becomes a further need, but even that need is undefined and unmet. And in our exhaustive quest, there is no exposure to the true and living God. For just as the hardened secularist can't point to God, the religious verbalist can't either. He points only to a concept. For God is beyond, outside and separate from us, hidden by the wants we see within ourselves. We are turned inward, and he is not there. We don't know that Omnipotent Other. We have, at best, only a poor sampling of him, filtered through a me-centered sighing that says, "This is what God means to *me*."

We have made Jesus to be *our* Jesus, and we are so accustomed to responding to "our" Jesus that we have forgotten how to respond to the Son of the living God.

His teachings have been taken with the pragmatic view of "getting it together," not followed because we must obey and can do nothing less. His words have been diluted by such diverse therapies as est and transcendental meditation so that all we know to respond to is a "feel-good" deity, a piece of religious plastic which we label "God."

We have found that even adding the adjective "Christian" doesn't change the noun, if the noun is "humanism." When we baptize the beliefs and practices of secular man, when we hold to them with the embrace of the committed, then nothing can change the fact that the ruling Lordship of Jesus Christ is missing from our actions and our thoughts.

For someone to reject God out of hand is one thing, but to acknowledge him and then live as if he is neither Lord nor God is a horrible existence. Then all we have left is sand.

God is ready to rescue us from ourselves, but that outstretched hand clutching at the sleeve is brushed aside with the scream, "Get your hands off me." God's Word replies, "O taste and see that the Lord is good: blessed is the man that trusteth in him" (Psalm 34:8, KJV). But we do not hear.

Yet because we can still think, we can still be healed. Life—real life with freedom—can still be found. We can still have friendship with God. We can still have the full life. But it must be a committed and disciplined life on God's terms.

God expects us to be disciplined. It is not the unnatural but rather the natural thing to be. We were created to be disciplined, put on this earth by God at this time and in this place not for personal gain or personal pleasure but for his purpose.

The "I've-only-got-one-try-so-I-will-go-for-it" syndrome, like any other orgy, is a suction into meaninglessness, and the vacuum from it draws in any who come near—even many who once acknowledged the words of Jesus, "Ye cannot serve God and mammon" (Matthew 6:24, KJV).

But we still have ears to hear, if we will. For into this scene comes Jesus saying, "A man's life consisteth not in the abundance of the things which he possesseth" (Luke 12:15, KJV).

"Do not be anxious for your life, as to what you shall eat; nor for your body, as to what you shall put on. For life is more than food, and the body than clothing" (Luke 12:22, 23, NASB).

"Do not seek what you shall eat, and what you shall drink, and do not keep worrying" (Luke 12:29, NASB).

"But seek for His kingdom, and these things shall be added to you" (Luke 12:31, NASB).

"Sell your possessions and give to charity; make yourselves purses which do not wear out, an unfailing treasure in heaven, where no thief comes near, nor moth destroys" (Luke 12:33, 34, NASB).

God is here in our world now. He has been all the time. He calls to scrambling, grasping people like us through the words of Jesus Christ. He says, "Come unto me."

It is time for us to do what he asks.

# TWO
# Winning

† *A bruised reed shall he not break, and the smoking flax shall he not quench* [Isaiah 42:3, KJV].

*Him that cometh to me I will in no wise cast out* [John 6:37, KJV].

Life is so ordinary.

And because it is, awakening to a daily practice of the disciplines of God is both exciting and liberating. For any who will seek it, there is a new freedom from those daily urgings that have become tyrants. Discipline is a freedom that comes not from taking or exploiting, but from *not* taking and *not* exploiting. In that freedom we become winners—each day, every day.

C. S. Lewis said, "A man who gives in to temptation after five minutes simply does not know what it would have been like an hour later. That is why bad people, in one sense, know very little about badness. They have lived a sheltered life by always giving in. We never find out the strength of the evil impulse inside us until we try to fight it."

Jesus was disciplined. He said, "For I came down from heaven, not to do mine own will, but the will of

27

him that sent me" (John 6:38, KJV).

Read the life of Christ in the New Testament, and as you do, keep asking one question over and over: "Was Jesus Christ happy?" What you discover will put your own happiness into focus. This happiness isn't what most of us think it is, nor is it what most of us have been striving for. It is deeper than that. With that realization and the determination to be like Jesus, we can change; we can take the road away from losing; we can find the winning way. It is God's way.

It starts with self-control. But our self-control is not, as many think, a control "of myself, by myself." Rather it is a matter of taking seriously what we know about ourselves, gathering up all that is "self," and yielding it to the rule of Christ. In this way we open up to the love and control of God. It is like a flower at dawn, touched by the warmth of the sun, opening to those sun rays and giving to the world its beauty, its perfume—being for all to see what it was meant to be. That is liberation; that is fulfillment at its highest. It is opposite to the way of the flesh, opposite to our own self-seeking, and opposite to failure.

In his book *In the Footprints of the Lamb,* G. Steinberger wrote, "Self-seeking will attempt only that which seems great, and will expect results only from persons of consequence. Its motto is: 'I feel that I am sufficient in myself. Everything must exist for me, otherwise it has no value.' But when love awakens in us, self-seeking dies; then the law of the flesh no longer rules, but the law of the spirit."

The disciplined life is a happy life. It is a controlled life. That is hard for many to understand, even those who say, "I am a Christian." For Christians are often the least disciplined, taking for their egos and their immediate needs the very things that stand in the way of enjoying and obeying God. Visit some of the Christian conferences or parachurch programs where Christians gather. Attend a meeting where a well-known Christian is the guest. The Christian jet set—dressed alike, talking alike, smiling alike, looking over the shoulders of the people with whom they are speaking in order to see who else has come into the room—all show how much they suffer from inferiority feelings which no child of God should harbor. Name dropping, each tries to impress the other; each takes what he can from a situation because he has nothing inside, nothing from God. Yet these same people tag what they do with the name of God because they "want to give him all the glory," even while they grab for what they hope will give them more personal, social, or even financial gain. They are boxed in, owned by the need for prestige, because they haven't learned how to let God be their all in all.

For too long most of us have thought that self-control was some form of punishment—a kind of masochism. That's not true. To indulge oneself not only destroys the spirit and body of a person, it destroys the sense of adventure and accomplishment that helps a person expand and grow. Self-control is probably one of the few frontiers that has never been fully conquered. For each of us it can become a new, exciting challenge.

I will never know what I can be with God until I try to live with him and for him. I need to know what I can resist, what I can do without, and what I can overcome. To work at this is as much a challenge as climbing Mount Everest or walking on the moon.

There is a real person inside each of us. That person

is more than a collection of genes, more than a jumble of experiences to be catalogued, more than a bottle of feelings to be uncorked and poured out. Each one of us is too wonderfully made to be reduced to such insignificance. We are much more than that.

God has made us with a profound complexity; we are mirrors of his image. We don't have to be victims of every whim that comes along. Discipline brings happiness. Discipline brings true fulfillment.

Self-controlled living says, "I will obey; I will follow not manmade attractions but God as he reveals himself in Jesus Christ, the Living Word, and in the Bible, the written Word." That is how happiness comes and that is how happiness stays. That kind of disciplined obedience holds its own rewards.

Yet even this can be twisted. It is shameful, but it happens. With our "instant" Christian mentality, we think that even discipline can be made easy and simple and practical. We search for some gimmick to make obedience fun, some formula we can memorize to help us to be disciplined, some austere, self-denying lifestyle we can put on like a coat. God won't be fooled by instant discipleship techniques or gimmicks. He knows that there can be just as much ego-centeredness in being "spiritual," just as much pride in austerity, and just as much dishonoring of God in what we do not do as there is in what we do. We can boast in our silence and seek one-upmanship over others in our pride as much as pagans can.

The instant-oriented, sensual Christian wants to "taste and see that the Lord is good" *now,* have all of his proffered blessings *now.* Such desires hold ulterior motives; he wants the windows of heaven open—

today. He wants what God gives more than he wants God.

Remember the often-quoted tithing story about the shovels? It is used to encourage people to give a tenth of their income to the Lord's work. Basically it is a proposition: "You shovel into God's bin, God will shovel into your bin, and God has the larger shovel." In other words, tithing is a sure-fire money-maker. You can't lose. "Give to God and he will give more back to you." But that's not true. More may *not* come back, nor does it have to come back. God is not in the negotiating business. He can and often will give "good measure, pressed down, and shaken together, and running over" (Luke 6:38, KJV). But he doesn't have to. It seems to be his loving nature to want to do so, but he does it because of who he is. No one bribes God to put into practice his being God.

The reality is this: if we take on the tithing discipline, we may have to do without. We may not be able to make payments on a new automobile or buy a boat. If we send gifts to missionaries, we may not also have money for entertainment. Tithing is a priorities proposition. It is based on obedience, not on wheeling and dealing with God. If God gives back to us more than we give, then that's his business. It is then his gift, an undeserved one, given for reasons that only he knows.

Any discipline is to be practiced for him because he asks us to do it. We agree to it because we don't want to disobey God. There is no demand that we can make of God for doing what we are expected to do.

The good Samaritan did not practice a "service-on-my-terms-if-it-suits-me-and-there-is-benefit-in-it-for-me" religion. The rules by which he lived were clear. He would help the sufferer. It cost him to do it, too, not only his time, but he probably got blood on his good suit. He left a deposit for the man's convalescence, then promised to pay the rest of the bill later. At no time did he ask for a receipt for income tax purposes, or for a *quid pro quo* from the beaten man.

Faithfulness and obedience are based on doing what we must do because we are committed to the One who asks us to do it. That's what we were created for.

We are entitled to true freedom, but entitled because he wants it for us. "Stand fast therefore in the liberty wherewith Christ hath made us free, and be not entangled again with the yoke of bondage" (Galatians 5:1 KJV). We are free! But we are free only in Christ. That's the paradox—there is liberty in discipline. We don't have to stay in our prisons of profligacy that we once misread as liberation. He wants us to be free *in his control*. That's real freedom, and we all can have it!

But it costs. We are so easily swept away in spite of our good intentions and resolves. Then we find ourselves down again, asking, "Will it always be like this? Can I never win against the world's control?" People who could be victorious find themselves little more than carbon copies of those who have never even tried to win. Instead of looking toward God, they look around, compare themselves to others, imitate, and end up feeling miserable.

That comparing and wanting is destructive. We should have known all along it would be, because Scripture shows that what is happening around us and to us is not new; it has happened to others.

The Bible lists examples of people who have looked around and made the wrong comparisons. And it shows what happened when they did. Cain compared himself with Abel—and killed him (Genesis 4:3–8). Esau compared himself with Jacob, caring nothing about what he had in his birthright—and ended up losing his inheritance (Genesis 25:30–34). Saul compared himself with David—and developed serious mental problems (1 Samuel 18:6–10).

We look at the athlete, the hero, the superstar, the one who has it all together or at least pretends that he has, and we try to copy him even though he is probably doing the same thing—copying someone else. We become envious, or, worse, jealous and morose. Finally we become angry with God. We deny how able he is to bless and fulfill and satisfy. And we lose. Because even if we succeed in getting all we want, become the person we envy in others, and say, "I've made it," we haven't made it at all.

Some 300 years ago, Richard Baxter described this mistake we keep making: "When we should study God, we study ourselves; when we should mind God, we mind ourselves; when we should love God, we love our carnal selves; when we should trust God, we trust ourselves; when we should honour God, we honour ourselves; and when we should ascribe to God, and admire Him, we ascribe to and admire ourselves: and instead of God we would have all men's eyes and dependence upon us, and all men's thanks returned to us, and would gladly be the only men on earth extolled and admired by all. And thus naturally we are our own idols."

Satan loves to have it that way. He works on any one of us—he did it with Jesus. When he began tempting Jesus on the mountain, there was no immediate intervention from the Father. Jesus had to struggle alone for forty days. Week in and week out he waited to be delivered. Deliverance didn't come. He could have taken the easy way, providing his own bread, rationalizing Satan's offer. He could have done that. He knew that it was possible. We do too. But to give in is failure. Jesus did not give in. He trusted the Father. He was obedient. Here, in the Son of God, our Savior, is our only true model.

But, unfortunately, the pattern we usually see around us is not the pattern of obedience but the pattern of independence and failure. Richard Lovelace states, "Much of the Christian community today is deeply penetrated by worldly patterns of thinking, motivation and behavior, and thus its spiritual life is deadened and its witness rendered ineffectual. Individuals, churches, schools and ministries must become sensitive to the areas of unholy conformity to the world in their behavior if the Spirit of holiness is really to possess them in fullness. But this is an awesome task, requiring an experience of the revelation of God's holiness and the depth of human sin like that which gripped Isaiah, who in his vision of God saw clearly not only his own sin but also the unclean lips of the people among whom he lived. Only this vision will motivate the world—and the church—to appropriate all the dimensions of life available in the fullness of Jesus Christ."

If we miss this appropriation of the fullness of Christ now, we could miss it again and again. We may never break out.

The Spirit of freedom, discipline, obedience, and holiness can possess us if our measure of what is good and desirable is God instead of what is touted by those who give no heed to his standards. There is an evil around us; it infects society and we are not to be a part of it. To compromise, to bring in the "me" perspective, is idolatry and it destroys.

G. Steinberger said, "The self-seeking soul is a robber, for he steals from God that which belongs to Him, and takes for himself that which belongs to others. Not only does self-seeking carry on its devilish work out in the world, but also in the gatherings of religious people, in the house of the righteous, even in the hearts of those who desire to follow the unselfish Jesus. It is self-seeking when one desires to appear more pious than others, to pray more beautifully than others, when one always wants to have the advantage for oneself. But the Scriptures say: 'Cursed be the deceiver' (Malachi 1:14)."

To the world in its darkness there is no choice, no other way to exist. But we who are in Christ do have another way, another choice. We can win. We must win. For to drift on into darkness brings us to failure before our God and others who would like to follow him and need help in order to do it. We must not fail those who are still in darkness and want a light by which they too can find their way out. If we are going to be any kind of light to a rebellious, disobedient, and undisciplined world, it will be only as we discipline ourselves under God's commands and allow him through us to demonstrate to the world that true experience of happiness that comes from obedience.

But if we slide farther and farther into the religion of the self, if we create a "friend in Jesus" who on *our terms* is going to fulfill whatever we ask, never mind the plan, the will, the purpose, the design, or even the privilege of Almighty God, then we have denied God. Like the sixteenth-century church people who trotted after John Tetzel when he used the slogan, "As soon as the coin in the coffer rings, the soul from purgatory springs," we trot after our made-up religion. It took the Reformation to turn people to what God wanted. That kind of reformation is due again, for so many still prefer to follow their Tetzels.

Richard Baxter asks: "If you tell others of the admirable joys of heaven, and yourselves do nothing but drudge for the world, and are as much taken up in striving to be rich, or as quarrelsome with your neighbors in a case of commodity, as any others, who will then believe you or who will be persuaded by you to seek the everlasting riches?"

Yes, who will believe?

So many who have taken his name have fallen away. They have come to the Light and have claimed the life-changing gifts of God's grace and peace, and then have surrendered them again, diving into the waters of sin, thinking that only in those waters will fulfillment come. Oh, how we cheapen his grace!

And many who claim the name but have not been living for him know that that is true. Winning will start when we come back to where we can hear his voice and determine to obey what he says.

It is like a waking-up, a coming back to life. It is that point where we say, "Enough." It is where we decide that we will follow Christ only and that we will not be bound by any other philosophy or agency or force. It is a renewing of our mind, a decision that we must be free and we will be free. We will move in the direction of the One who owns us, the Lord Jesus Christ. It is a vow we make, a promise that we will accept, whatever sacrifice is necessary in order to be free. For each one of us, it is a decision: "I must have him. I will have him."

The Christian disciple will obey. There is no law or structure to demand it; the disciple's obedience is built on a love that calls him to hear and to do what the Master asks.

Have you told God yet that you love him? Have you told him yet that you are willing to obey him?

What are you waiting for?

As we come closer to that predicted day when "men shall be lovers of their own selves" (2 Timothy 3:2, KJV), each of us has to decide: Even if I am the only one, I will live a life of faithfulness and obedience.

Many will be coming to this late in life. We cannot undo our undisciplined years. We cannot give back what we have already taken, nor rebuild what our rebellion has destroyed. We cannot fully heal what we have hurt. But we can begin again now, and God wants us to. He makes possible the new beginning. He is the giver of our desire for obedience and the rewarder of our attempts at the disciplined life. Obedience to discipline is built on trust, and he does bless those who trust him. Scripture states, "Blessed is that man that maketh the Lord his trust" (Psalm 40:4, KJV).

When that simple winning choice is made, the forward steps begin. At last each of us can say, "I don't have to be a victim any more. Before God I can live out a holy, obedient, and disciplined life. I can start over. I *will* start over."

# THREE
## Starting Over

† *"For I know the plans I have for you," declares the Lord, "plans to prosper you and not to harm you, plans to give you hope and a future. Then you will call upon me and come and pray to me, and I will listen to you. You will seek me and find me when you seek me with all your heart. I will be found by you," declares the Lord, "and will bring you back from captivity. I will gather you from all the nations and places where I have banished you," declares the Lord, "and will bring you back to the place from which I carried you into exile"* [Jeremiah 29:11–14, NIV].

Haven't you had enough?

There is a time for coming back to discipline, self-control, and a life lived on God's terms. Now is that time. We have been through it all—the grasping, the looking, the searching. We have lived as people who try to serve God and mammon, and we know now that it cannot be done. Friendship with God and friendship with that which is not of God just cannot be.

It is time to turn away from the mix of God's Word plus my opinions, God's orders plus my wants, God's love plus my lusts, and turn back to a true commitment. For many, the heresy of these mixtures isn't even obvious. It will become obvious only when the concern to be obedient and the love for the Word become consuming passions. A. W. Tozer urged: "Come near to the holy men and women of the past and you will soon feel the heat of their desire after God. They mourned for Him, they prayed and wrestled and sought for Him day and night, in season and out, and when they had found Him the finding was all the sweeter for the long seeking. Moses used the fact that he knew God as an argument for knowing Him better. 'Now, therefore, I pray thee, if I have found grace in thy sight, show me now thy way, that I may know thee, that I may find grace in thy sight'; and from there he rose to make the daring request, 'I beseech thee, show me thy glory.' God was frankly pleased by this display of ardor, and the next day called Moses onto the mount, and there in solemn procession made all His glory pass before him.

"David's life was a torrent of spiritual desire, and his psalms ring with the cry of the seeker and the glad shout of the finder. Paul confessed the mainspring of his life to be his burning desire after Christ. 'That I may know him,' was the goal of his heart, and to this he sacrificed everything. 'Yea doubtless, and I count all things but loss for the excellency of the knowledge of Christ Jesus my Lord: for whom I have suffered the loss of all things, and do count them but refuse, that I may win Christ.'"

Perhaps most of the people you know will not turn back; most may keep right on in the same old way. But that shouldn't matter to you. You can't wait to see what the trend will be. You know that you've followed the world long enough. You know the emptiness of trying to find your happiness in ways other than those God offers. You know from experience that those other ways don't work.

Most of us have watched people who have gone to extremes in ways that are not God's ways. We have seen the result of absorbing values that are loose, weak, undisciplined, and unbiblical. Now we can see, even apart from all the scriptural warnings that should have helped us to see sooner, where uncontrolled living goes. We know the misery. We have seen it; many of us have felt it. Now we come to the point where we say, "No more!" With Joshua we say, "Choose . . . this day whom ye will serve," and then we stand, even if we are the only ones to do so, and declare, "As for me and my house, we will serve the Lord" (Joshua 24:15, KJV).

This is not an easy commitment to make. For some it won't even come from great conviction. It will come, frankly, from the pain of having gone the other route, the mammon route, and finding nothing there. It will come because at last we will have looked at ourselves and said, "Oh, God, why does so much seem so wrong? What is happening?" And we will know that we have come to the turning point.

We turn back not because God has punished us. He hasn't; he has simply allowed us to dig our own holes and fall into them. As we have fallen, he has allowed it. When we said "no" to his pity and his offer of rescue, he did not force himself upon us. We wanted him to leave us alone, and he did. But he has always been ready to ask again, "Haven't you had enough?"

F. P. Harton wrote in his book *The Elements of the Spiritual Life,* "As the sense of one's own insufficiency deepens, as one realizes that one's failures in the spiritual life are the result of one's own faults or weakness, and not of the failure of grace, so one is able to abandon oneself to the sufficiency of God."

Each one of us knows when and if he has reached that time of personal realization: "I'm at a dead end." Each of us knows when he is ready to turn fully to God. But even if you think that time has come for you now, be careful of what you agree to before God. Don't come to him just for a warm glow or a feeling of euphoria. Don't come to him for success or miracles or man's praise. If you do, you won't stay with him. Come to be a disciple.

But you had better be quiet and inconspicuous about it. Don't wear a button declaring that Jesus is now the master of your life. Just let him be Master. Don't call a press conference to tell the world that you are "pro-Jesus." Satan knows your weaknesses. He knows how to trip you. Just follow Jesus. Give an account for your obedience when asked, tell people the Good News, point to Christ, but when you do that, get yourself out of the way. You are entering God's business, and it isn't a game.

But be prepared. You'll still be seduced by the appeals that attempt to connect real living to cosmetic and plastic pleasures. There will still be packaged pretty people generating insecurity in you by pushing you toward something else—whether it's a new lifestyle, a new theology, or a new deodorant. They will still tell you that you don't have to look the way you look; you don't have to dress the way you dress; you needn't drive what you drive, or do without, or exercise self-control, or use the Bible as your guide. You will still be offered ways to live on tomorrow's earnings, to take more and give less. You will still be

urged to modify biblical injunctions to suit your pleasure, to justify an easier lifestyle. Expect it to happen.
Conquer it!

Know that this pressure will come. Give it over to
God. Any stick of wood can drift downstream, but it
takes someone determined and alive to swim up-
stream. Richard Foster says in *Celebration of Discipline,* "Refuse to be a slave to anything but God."
The Apostle Paul said to people greatly influenced by
their culture and society, "I beseech you therefore,
brethren, by the mercies of God, that ye present your
bodies a living sacrifice" (Romans 12:1, KJV). He is
begging us by God's mercies, not our merits, to be
"living" perpetual sacrifices, not something transient
or occasional. We are to purposefully surrender completely to God. As a living gift, we turn over to God
all that we are and all that he put into us—our abilities, our thoughts, our strengths. And as living sacrifices, offered as presents, we are to be holy and
acceptable, pure and unblemished, just as the ancient
animal sacrifices were.

How can this be? Both our holiness and our accept-
ability are his doing, his act of grace. We will have it
if we claim the offered gift of it through the redeeming, transforming transaction at the cross. Jesus
Christ paid for our sins and destroyed their consequences. And we receive the gift of gifts from him:
his life, eternal life, a post-grave life. In response, this
presentation of our bodies—head, heart, hands—is
our worship. We owe him this.

We should know, then, that this is what worship
is—a presentation of ourselves in whom he delights.
Following an order of service in church is worship
only if it is a part of that self-presentation. For neither

songs nor sermons nor liturgy nor prayer is worship unless it is part of and comes out of that giving of the only present we can give—ourselves, a living sacrifice, holy and acceptable.

And the point is that we are no longer to be conformed to the world as unrenewed people are. No one who is in Christ Jesus can be the same as one who is not. We who are in Christ are different. We have begun a new process. Do not continue to grow into conformity with the world, the Apostle says, but be transformed. We are to be transfigured by the renewing of our minds. This is an act that involves the mind; we are transformed by a lasting change as we think it through, weigh it, and say yes. Then we can be—indeed we will be—in the business of proving in our lives the perfect will of God. Day by day we will do this, committed to being proof for all to see of what is the good, perfect, and acceptable will of God.

Is that what you're ready to do?

As a child who has placed his hand in the hand of his father, the Christian walks into new life in Christ knowing that God is in control. He enters with an awareness that God is God. He knows he cannot understand God's total will. The Father knows what lies ahead; the Christian is asked to go with him. There is no other way for obedience to be practiced.

This is not blindness on our part; this is coming to grips at last with the reality of knowing who we are and who he is. It is knowing who made us, who owns us, and what we are worth by the purchase of Jesus Christ. A. H. McNeile said, "The only way in which to know ourselves better is to know Christ better, and to be constantly comparing ourselves, not with other people but, with Him."

It is believed that Job was the first book of Scripture to be written, and is therefore the oldest book in the Bible. If that is true, then it is interesting that the very first book written isn't about blessing. It is about afflictions and pain that became so unbearable that Job's wife told him to curse God and die. Job refused; he cursed the day he was born, he wished he had never lived, but he refused to curse God and die. Job is a testimony to faithfulness no matter what happens in life.

Some me-oriented people, starting from their own perspective rather than God's, look at Job and say, "But Job was blessed later on." That's true, for God is gracious. But during the time of suffering and faithfulness Job didn't know he would ultimately be blessed. He trusted God not because he expected that God would give back more than he took; he trusted because he knew that God was God. In his suffering and misery he believed God.

Job did not even have what we have to go on; he did not have the example of a previous Job. He had to face his life without such a biblical example to help him. But because he did, we have his example to help us today. Whatever we face, whatever good or bad comes, we know what faithfulness is—we have watched Job.

The first and only reason for obedience is because God is God. There are no secret agendas when we throw ourselves on the altar as living sacrifices. We don't make demands of God. If we could, he would be too small. He would be our size. But he is the God beyond and above all of us, yet involved totally with us, with an understanding of our todays that is way beyond our own understanding, and with knowledge of tomorrows which are already in his hands.

Look at Joseph. When he was sold as a slave into Egypt, could he have known what God had ordained for the future? There was no way for him to know, yet in his faithfulness he worked at becoming the best man he could be for God. And God honored that. Though others meant Joseph's slavery for evil, God used it for his larger plan. Joseph was faithful to God long before anything good happened in his life. And since he did not know what we know now about the latter part of his life, we have to assume that he would have remained faithful even if he had died without ever knowing the ultimate purpose or plan of God for his situation.

Stephen the Apostle died and did not know about his influence on Saul of Tarsus. He did not demand, "Tell me, God, how my death is a good thing for the Christian church." No, he endured stoning for his faith and died a horrible death. How God used Stephen's death for his glory, was determined later. We are blessed today because of Stephen's faithfulness then.

Look at what Moses and his people faced at the hands of Pharaoh. Ultimately the suffering was what brought the people of Israel out of Egypt and produced a great nation, a people from whom would come the Messiah, our Lord Jesus Christ. But did Moses know all that at the time? Did Moses understand Pharaoh's role in his life?

What about the pharaohs in your life? What about the people who make your life difficult now when you try to be obedient to God, the ones who make your commitment to God an excuse to try to crush you even more? You may suffer as a disciplined follower, and you may ask why. But God may not answer you because he doesn't have to answer you. What is happening to you may be for a reason far greater than you could ever imagine. Your trouble with a pharaoh or your wilderness wandering may be the prelude to a great act of God. Your responsibility is to be obedient to what you know and to move through life with God.

One night while reading a publication from England, I came upon an article about the Archbishop of Canterbury, the Most Reverend Robert Runcie. I took out a pad of paper and wrote an editorial for *Decision* magazine. In it I said, "What caught my attention was the honesty with which this man of God spoke about his spiritual growth and especially his comment about his days as a student and in military service. He said, 'I was taken more with Christians than Christianity.'

"That struck me because I've drawn some personal comfort (and actually made excuses for myself) by thinking that people shouldn't look at me, they should ignore me and look at Christ. That's fine to say, but the fact is that people do as Robert Runcie did. They look at Christians, not the Church, not even Christ.

"The young man who would become Archbishop liked what he saw, so much so that he was inspired to do more decisive thinking about the Christian faith. When a fellow university student who had been preparing for the ministry was killed in the war, the parents of that young man said, 'We have come to terms with our son's death because we know that God likes the buds as well as the full flowers.' Today the Archbishop looks back to that young man and his parents and those words as the means God used in motivating him toward his own preparation for the ministry.

"As I finished reading the interview, I asked myself, 'Does the way I live my life attract people to Jesus Christ? If I were to die soon, would my death lead others to go on in the Faith and perhaps do more than I could ever do for Christ and his Kingdom?'

"The influence of one person upon another cannot be lightly dismissed. Maybe 'my great work' is to be an influence that God uses to bring someone else to himself, someone who will truly do 'great things for God.'

"What really counts is living without guile or pretense and trusting to God the witness of the life we live. Forty years ago one faithful young man did. The result of his brief life and the response of his parents to his death caused another young man to embark on a spiritual journey that led . . . to his enthronement as the Archbishop of Canterbury."

Whom are you influencing now by your faithfulness? Conversely, whom may you be influencing away from God by your search for a bargain-counter God? No matter how difficult our path seems, God knows what he is doing when he calls us to obedience and discipline.

Will you pledge to try not to outthink God or run ahead of God? In his book *In The Footprints of the Lamb,* G. Steinberger said, "Only he who has committed himself to Him can surrender himself to Him. One gives himself to God only once, but one commits himself consciously from day to day, and thus one learns to surrender himself to God."

"Why me, God?" Better to ask, "Why not me?" Are you better than others of the faith? Are you better than a Moses or a Joseph or a Job or even a John the Baptist? You will consume hours, even years, of creative energy if you spend them worrying about why something is happening to you. When you believe in God, you need not worry. If you believe in the economy of God, you will know that he wastes nothing. He knows what he is doing in your life at every moment. He knows why you are here and what your purpose is, and why he put you on this earth with your gifts and your talents and all that makes you what you are. He knows why you live at this time and in this place, with all that is happening around you. David knew that and said so in Psalm 139. You are no accident. All the buffeting and pulling and tearing that happens is not without meaning. God may not cause some things, but he allows them, and the overall plan that guides a committed life is under his control.

A. H. McNeile has told us what it is to live by the light and rule of God: "We are only instruments, implements, tools for the building of God's temple. Some people are like the tools fitted for the delicate and delightful work of carving or painting. They have the joy, by their very touch, of converting and beautifying souls. Some, who are able to start great schemes and engineer important movements, are like the powerful cranes that lift masses of masonry into their places. But others, and probably we amongst them, are to do spadework in digging foundations; or we are to be like the humble trowel that slowly adds brick after brick, or the humble hammer that patiently hits nail after nail, or the humble nail itself, firmly fixed in a sure place, invisible, but doing one little piece of work well. . . .

"The musician wants something different from the violin, the cello, the cornet, and every other instrument in the orchestra; and yet each can express quite fully what he wants from that particular instrument. S. Jerome put it in stirring words when he said that Christ wants from us 'not impossibilities but perfections.' It is impossible for me to express to God what He wants from you. But His ideal is that I should give to Him perfectly what He wants from me. It will save us endless trouble if we grasp that clearly. It will save us from the feeling that it must be easier for so-and-so to please God than for me. If I only had his chances! If I only had his temperament, or upbringing, his surroundings, his friends, his religious privileges, his sphere of work; or his voice, or command of language, or appearance. He is so rich in natural gifts, and I seem to have almost none; I'm a most dreadfully ordinary person. And perhaps in weak moments you have gone so low as to say, He has heaps of money, and I have very little; how can I do as much for God as he can? Perhaps you have gone even lower still, and said, God will make it up to me hereafter, and give me things that he won't have! All this, and many more of the doubts and grumbles that sometimes pass through our minds, come from forgetting the plain, obvious truth that if God had made you different from what you are, He would have wanted something different from you."

No matter how Satan prowls and torments and tortures and hurts us, no matter how we suffer (and we will because we are a part of a fallen world and part of the decay that leads to the end), as long as we are committed to Christ we are always his. We are to measure our lives against his reality, not against our ideals which are only fantasies.

Being under the discipline of God, then, is not an easy life, but it's a *real* life. It is a life that redefines the meaning of pleasure. It is a life that will redefine *you,* your significance in the world, and your purpose on earth.

Haven't you had enough of the indulgent life? Isn't it time to come back to discipline and a life lived on God's terms?

# FOUR
# Another Way to Live

† *Ye are my friends, if ye do whatsoever I command you. Henceforth I call you not servants . . . but I have called you friends* [John 15:14, 15, KJV].

Something is happening to someone close to you, but you may not have noticed yet. There is a person less anxious than those around him, someone with a quiet purpose to his life. He understands the meaning of faithfulness, obedience, control; he has discovered a deeper satisfaction than other people pull out of the shallow gratifications of the immediate. He is a person who is able not to take just because the taking is available. He does not feel sorry for himself when someone else "gets there" first. This person is different. He refuses to look at life with the narrow view, the view that says, "I'm entitled to satisfaction and pleasure or anything else that I want—and I will have it." He is bigger than that. He is a person who has learned another way to live. Particularly—and contentedly—he has learned to live a disciplined life. And he likes himself because he can.

This is the person who, when suffering, resolves to endure.

This is the one who reads the marriage manuals

that advise, "You have a right to divorce and remarriage," and still answers, "No, I don't."

This is the person who, like Joseph in Egypt, will go without companions and emotional support if necessary but still refuses to give way to the temptations around him.

He is the one who can say to others who urge him to take his "rights," "I'll go without."

Are people like this mentally unbalanced? Are they masochists?

Or are these a people who have discovered a stronger, more satisfying support structure for living?

They have! They have found not just a cause or a system. But they have thought through the implications of what Oxford don C. S. Lewis said: "If you are thinking of becoming a Christian, I warn you you are embarking on something which is going to take the whole of you." And they have decided to do it. They have accepted the warning and have gained the results.

These are committed followers of Jesus Christ, and they are off on a different adventure. They are the sheep who have heard his voice and have chosen to obey him. Jesus said, "My sheep . . . follow me" (John 10:27, KJV)—and they do. Richard Lovelace describes what they are and what they have: "True spirituality is not a superhuman religiosity; it is simply true humanity released from bondage to sin and renewed by the Holy Spirit." That is their secret. But it doesn't have to be a secret. It's available to all of us.

We too can be a people who understand what it means to belong to Jesus Christ. We too can determine to follow and obey him. Each of us can be a person who has chosen to live out his life in the pleasure of his company. James H. McConkey explains: "What we are becomes the measure of what we can do or, rather, what God can do through us. We must be Christ-like in inner life, if we would be Christ-like in outward deed. A holy God needs a holy instrument through which to live His holy life."

Holiness means health. The holy person is a healthy person. The person who is not holy is unwell. It isn't normal to want to be unwell. It is normal to want to be healthy. The friends of God, the obedient ones, the disciplined followers, have found health.

But this is not simply a lifestyle that one adopts or a set of religious rules to try to obey. This is a response. It is a yes to the One who prefaced his teaching with, "If anyone will come after me. . . ."

In churches, in neighborhood groups, by one's and two's, people are sorting out what that means and scraping away the corroding barnacles of existential-ism and humanism which have dragged all of us down for so long. They are chucking the theological adjuncts in favor of dependency on God. And to the best of their ability, prayerfully and devotionally they are becoming people who follow him. The French philosopher Emile Cailliet described it: "New Testa-ment Christianity lives on, lives on with all the rough hedges of the Apostolic Proclamation, lives on with all the foolishness of its otherworldliness. When the theologians and natural scientists have done their best, or their worst, this fact is still there, staring them in the face."

The life of discipleship is the life of living as a friend of God. It is not immediately an easy road to choose, and many won't choose it. Most people will play along the fringe, trying to get a little of the light and warmth of God without walking with him and abiding in him. There will always be people, peripheral believers, superficial adherents, who take the stumbling-along view that says, "Each of us is free to decide the conditions under which God expects us to obey him." Worse, there will always be those people who simply back out if a promise made to God seems to be no longer viable. But not all will do that. Some have learned.

A college student explained, "She came to me right at the time when I didn't think I could take much more—the pressure from my parents, the financial strain, the classwork demands. I needed an out, even a temporary escape. Then I felt her touch on my arm. 'You're really tense,' she said. 'Would you like me to help you relax?' I didn't know her except as another member of the class but apparently she had been watching me. She saw my need and she made her offer. She meant it; there was genuine kindness in her sympathetic tone. But I couldn't. I said, with appreciation for her thoughtfulness, 'No, thank you,' and I walked away."

He didn't preach at her or criticize. How could he criticize kindness? Neither did he refuse her offer because he had some "better" release for his tensions. He had none. He was alone. There was no one else on the horizon offering him any different kind of help, a help that he would and could accept.

He went without. He said no to the caring that she offered, with nothing to replace it. He endured without a release.

Is he unhealthy? Is he foolish? Doesn't he know that bottled-up feelings and emotional stress can bring greater tension? Maybe. But so does temporary escape, regardless of the form. He knows that too. The clear word that God gave is still there in front of all of us, and that student had it. "I will *never* leave thee, nor forsake thee" (Hebrews 13:5, KJV). For that, and that alone, he held on until God's help came. He responded to her not by feeling or even by blind faith. He acted by wisdom. "The fear of the Lord is the beginning of wisdom" (Psalm 111:10, KJV). Wisdom doesn't end with the fear of God, but without the fear of God it doesn't begin.

It is in the everyday events of life when people like that student prove whether or not they will be obedient. Holiness is a behavior as well as a belief. It isn't the difference between "criminal" and "law-abiding." It is the difference between good and best. We practice holiness because of friendship with God. There is no semifriendship, no occasional fear of the Lord.

I know two men who work for a nonprofit organization. Both travel on expense accounts. One lives as a friend of God; the other does not. Circumstances are the same for both, but their responses to those circumstances are opposite. This is how the difference shows:

"Go ahead and order the steak."

"But I don't eat like this at home; I can't afford it."

"You're not at home; it's going on your expense account."

"No."

"You work hard; you've earned it."

"I'm paid to work hard. I am not paid to exploit."

When those two men started their work, both had strong convictions about the high calling of their vocation. They felt a sense of mission in a worthwhile organization, one that helped people in need. They kept costs down so that the money could be used as the donors expected it to be used. But then they began to notice that others in their group weren't so fussy. After awhile it became easier for one of those men to change from a high view of commitment to the rationalization, "You won't be appreciated any more if you don't take." Even worse, he gave in to the charge, "You make the rest of us look bad when we turn in our expenses."

Now that man thinks this way: "Others are looking out for themselves; why should I be so virtuous? The money I don't spend on myself doesn't provide more for those in need, it just provides more for the others in the organization who do look out for themselves." So now he has joined the others. He is spending more on himself too.

But the other man won't bend. He says, "When you see poor people who are willing to give a dollar in order to help someone else, that stays with you. You can't spend that money on yourself." He can't do it, and he won't do it. It means fighting against a trend, and he fights it everyday. The other man doesn't have to fight anymore; he has already given in. For him there is no longer a battle. For the disciplined man the battle continues; it probably always will. He isn't even feeling good about it. And he isn't announcing, "You're wrong; I'm right." He just goes on, one day at a time, trying to do what is expected of him by God.

And usually that's all we have to go on if we are trying to be a friend of God. What others say cannot be the measure of what is ethical, moral, or right, even if it is legal. The view of the majority is not necessarily the view of God.

I know a woman whose husband has been seducing other women for years. She could get a divorce; she has been encouraged by her friends to do it. But she won't. She's not trying to be a martyr or heroine; she's not trying to bring more pain into her life for some kind of self-inflicted psychological punishment. She made a vow to God: "For better or worse," and she meant that vow. The sacred commitment was not only in the words she spoke but in the promise behind those words. Believing that God heard her when she made that promise, she is going to stand on it and seek God's help to implement that promise whether or not his help comes according to her own timetable, or even to the degree of personal satisfaction that she would like to have.

Her stance is so different from that taken by the rest of our culture that to many people it seems incomprehensible. "How can she do what she is doing?" they exclaim. She hears the arguments: "You are the innocent party." "Don't you want a better life?" "Think of your children." "If divorce is wrong, it isn't the worst wrong; God forgives." "You aren't getting any younger." "You have a responsibility to yourself." "God is love and wants you to be loved." Then comes that often used line: "God wants you to be happy."

But she already knows all of those arguments. She has heard them over and over again. She has thought them through and has made up her mind.

Even Christians who accept her view and admit that she is probably correct, or who praise her glowingly, turn to look for some compensation from God to be granted to her for her faithfulness. But no reward has come. Life is still miserable for her. So then fellow Christians too begin to argue with her: "If God expected you to endure such suffering, at least he would have given you some other blessing to reward you."

But she responds, "Why should he?"

And she explains again, "I obey my pledge because I promised that I would obey my pledge. Why should God be expected to give me some great reward for doing what I promised to do in the first place? I said, 'For better or worse.' God was there when I said it, and God hasn't moved away. And no matter how my husband has drifted, or for whatever reason, God is with me now. Would I divorce my husband if instead of losing his head to other women he lost his mind to a disease?"

She has kept her vow, even though there are still people coming around to remind her that times have changed, her world has changed, her husband has changed, and she has changed. She remembers what they have chosen to forget: God *hasn't* changed—and her promise was made to God.

The faithful ones, the vow-keepers, the disciplined people of God, are not some new kind of standard-bearers. They are simply people who have chosen to be consistent in the adventure of following Jesus. They aren't trying to be different or strange. They are not looking for personal suffering. They are not drawing attention to themselves: "Look at all that I'm doing and all that I'm giving up." They want to enjoy life, the pleasures of home and good health. But whether they have the "good" or the "bad," they *will* follow Jesus. And they will do it faithfully, wherever that obedience leads. They, like St. Paul, know how to be abased as well as how to abound (Philippians 4:12), and will be abased if that is what is required within their commitment to obedience. They will be what their Lord has asked—faithful. And if there is some primary word about being a friend of God, it is that word—"faithful." Everything else is secondary. For each friend of God, the decision comes to that!

Jesus did not come to this earth in order to call a few selected disciples to a happy three-year vacation from routine. Nor did he bring a mission of blessing to make people comfortable. He came to obey his Father. That led to a cross. There was no alternative for our redemption but that cross. If there had been, God would not have sent his Son—it was so costly. But he did send his Son, and Jesus obeyed his Father's will. What if Jesus had chosen the more pleasant way of remaining with his Father? Or, once Incarnate, what if he had decided that the situation had changed or the responsibility was too severe? What if he had said no to the cross?

Are Jesus' disciples to take liberties, playing fast and loose with God the Father in the name of him who would not and could not disobey? Do we say yes or no depending on how we feel in a given situation or moment? Are there no firm orders for the one who claims to be a follower of him who "stedfastly set his face" (Luke 9:51, KJV), who from the beginning knew that he had to work the works of him who sent him (see John 9:4, KJV)?

Those who choose to follow the Master do so on his terms. It is obedience with no reservation clause added to the contract. There is no back door left ajar

so that we can slip out when the mood strikes or feelings change. "Ye are my friends," Jesus said, "if ye do
whatsoever I command you" (John 15:14, KJV). We
are to be obedient even if we never see "good results"
from it. The measure of what is "good" is not ours to
make.

There is always the human tendency to look down
the road, to ask, "How will all this turn out for me,
for the kingdom, or for others?" We try to figure it all
out. Even when following means martyrdom, we
tend to look at it for its long-range effect. Dietrich
Bonhoeffer, the German pastor killed by the Nazis in
1945, did not look for prison and eventual death, nor,
if he saw it coming, did he look for its long-range
effect on others. He just obeyed God.

To the question, "What if my obedience doesn't
turn out well?" we have to respond, "What if it
doesn't?"

"What if I make a mistake?"

Well, what if you do? God wants your obedience.
Scripture tells us that "whosoever believeth on him
shall not be ashamed" (Romans 10:11, KJV). What
comes to us as a result of our trust in God is God's
responsibility, not ours. We are not worriers about
tomorrow either for ourselves or for our witness to
the kingdom. We do not have to anticipate the plan of
God and help him develop it.

People who are being martyred today because they
are Christians do not see their deaths as a witness to
Christ—all they see is death coming. There is no
last-minute realization, "I am a blessed martyr and
thus others will come to Christ." There is no last-
minute, glorious, divine intervention to ease the pain
of bullets or blade. There is none of that for them.

But they are faithful anyway. They have to be because they are his. That's what it is to be a friend of God.

Ultimately the person who says yes to Jesus Christ has to know that he is making a decision, choosing an option to obey, following whether there are great rewards in it or none, whether it is for good or for suffering, life or death. Some summertime believers will do without for awhile if God will provide blessings for them in the end. But God may not. And the committed disciple doesn't question that. He knows he must go on even through long spiritual winters.

Any person who has not made this commitment to Jesus Christ will be totally confused, even angry, at this explanation of true friendship with God. That's to be expected. He won't—indeed he can't—understand. "The natural man receiveth not the things of the Spirit of God: for they are foolishness unto him" (1 Corinthians 2:14, KJV). Those immature, unbelieving people are wrong if they presume obedience is simple self-denial—an ascetic, masochistic way of life. Self-negation is not at all what obedience means. The person who goes without something in order to be noticed or who becomes a martyr by his own doing is still seeking a reward—and as Jesus said of the hypocrites who blew their trumpets, "They have their reward" (Matthew 6:2, KJV). Those who impose on themselves the ascetic, self-denying life do so on *their* terms—it is merely a religious facade. It is not real obedience to Jesus. God's call for us to deny ourselves doesn't stop there; it has a purpose, being linked to his call for us to *follow him*.

Jesus said, "If any man will come after me, let him deny himself, and take up his cross, and follow me"

(Matthew 16:24, KJV). That means exactly what Jesus says it means—follow him! It doesn't mean that *I* decide to live on a smaller income, but I will if *he* decides it for me. It doesn't mean that *I* surrender my house, but I will if *he* wishes it. It doesn't mean that *I* choose to face a firing squad or the persecution of my neighbors, but I will if that's where *obedience* takes me.

It has to be that way because in coming to him I am purposely and willingly choosing to yield my body as a living sacrifice, "holy and pleasing to God—which is . . . worship" (Romans 12:1, NIV). I am no longer my own; I am bought with a price—the price of the Lord Jesus Christ. I am paid for. The Christian is a disciple; more accurately, he is a chosen vessel "unto honour, sanctified, and meet for the master's use, and prepared unto every good work" (2 Timothy 2:21, KJV).

That's what is so different about this adventure called friendship with God. There is neither heroics nor fame to it, no cheers from the crowd; there is no recognition in biographies; no motion pictures are filmed. It is a choice to walk quietly but faithfully beside Jesus even while all around the noise of the market of worldliness attracts, while those who are avoiding Jesus, seeming to live comfortably and well in their unbelief, are smirking and saying under their breath, "What a fool."

But we are not fools; we are discoverers of a new and stirring life. As Thomas Kelly explained, "Deep within us all there is an amazing inner sanctuary of the soul, a holy place, a Divine Center, a speaking Voice, to which we may continuously return. Eternity is at our hearts, pressing upon our time-torn lives, warming us with intimations of an astounding destiny, calling us home unto itself. Yielding to these persuasions, gladly commiting ourselves in body and soul, utterly and completely, to the Light Within, is the beginning of true life. . . . It is a Light within which illumines the face of God and casts new shadows and new glories upon the face of men. It is a seed stirring to life if we do not choke it. It is the Shekinah of the soul, the Presence in the midst. Here is the Slumbering Christ, stirring to be awakened, to become the soul we clothe in earthly form and action. And He is within us."

The disciple determines that he must have what God wants for him. Nothing less will do. This means he cannot and will not give in to the temptations that dissipate and hurt and destroy. There is too much at stake. His very being and welfare—his full life—is at stake. He only has one life to enjoy on this earth. Why should he use it to run after what can never satisfy? Why should he give his one life to anything less than the wholeness, the purity, the love, and the joy of God?

Why would he want to work so hard for a few years to gain what "moth and rust will corrupt," what "thieves will break through and steal," when he can have so much more that will never corrupt or decay? Why would he not want the eternal investments now and the dividends of those investments forever? Ephesians 1:4 says: "He hath chosen us . . . that we should be holy and without blame before him" (KJV). Then, why not?

What can this friendship with God fully mean? Do any of us really know what it is to be holy, to be blameless, to be loved? We know a little of it, but there is so much more of it to know—and he calls us to discover it all.

God wants you near him and wants lovingly to guide your life. There is still that one clear certainty in an age when nothing else is certain at all: God wants you to be his friend. He wants to give you the pleasure of his company.

Long ago, God said through Elijah, "How long will you waver between two opinions? If the Lord is God, follow him" (1 Kings 18:21, NIV). It is time to heed that call again. If we have forsaken or compromised the disciplines of faithfulness, we have made the wrong choice. It is time to come back, to start over.

Start a life of holy obedience now; start where you are, as you are. Whether or not others do it, start. There is no better time. Tell God you are ready—tell him now. You can say your yes to God because, at last, to everything else you can say no!

# F I V E
# At Last! I Can Say No

† *As obedient children, do not conform to the evil de-*
*sires you had when you lived in ignorance. But just as*
*he who called you is holy, so be holy in all you do*
[1 Peter 1:14, 15, NIV].

Hans Rookmaaker, the Dutch expert in art history
and a disciplined Calvinist, felt deep pain when he
learned that a friend had left his wife to live with another woman. Rookmaaker was shocked that this
man believed that he could do it as a Christian because
"the Gospel gives me freedom." Rookmaaker's biog-
rapher quotes: "I told him that unless things drasti-
cally changed he is not seen anymore as a Christian by
me. I want to remain friends, but not within the
Christian group."

Someone may say, "That's cruel! We have to live in
this world, and the world is not ideal. There are
temptations and struggles; none of us is perfect. Who
has a right to judge another?" The answer is, God has
that right. Isaiah said, "Woe unto them that call evil
good, and good evil; that put darkness for light, and
light for darkness; that put bitter for sweet, and sweet
for bitter!" (Isaiah 5:20, KJV).

God knows our world. In Jesus Christ he entered

the world and was tempted in all points as we, yet without sin. He is the one who said, "Take up your cross and follow me." It is not an easy weight, that cross. He never promised that it would be an easy cross to bear or a pretty one to display or one that would bring excitement or pleasure.

We don't have to bear the cross if we don't want to. We can refuse, or worse, say that we will take up the cross knowing full well that we won't. We can be like the son who said to his father, "Yes, I will go into the vineyard," but didn't. We can say that, but we will answer for that kind of lying. We can filter the commands of God through our own system of wants and desires and "needs" if we want to, but we will stand before him and give an account for what we have done. All these things will be "uncovered and laid bare before the eyes of him to whom we must give account" (Hebrews 4:13, NIV).

He knows where we are and what we face. He knows where he has placed us. He knows also that we don't have to slip and slide and fall. The mud pits of this world do not have to be entered. We can say no.

An easing of the commandments a little here, the acceptance of something less than the best there is of our own making; we slide by our own choice. The giving in to personal desires is not his doing, it is ours.

William Barclay had it right when he said, "Once a thing is not forbidden, it may be felt not only to be permitted but to be encouraged. It could be argued that what the law does not permit, it approves." We move from permission to acceptance, and our acceptance becomes a form of insistence: "This is my right." "This fulfills me!" And I become my own law, my own God.

In the fourth and fifth centuries in Egypt there were religious people who recognized the dangers of the self-indulgent life. They did something about it. They became monks. We can learn something valuable from them and from the whole monastic movement.

Some may criticize those ancient monks for their theological weaknesses such as not fully understanding salvation by faith in Christ alone. But we can't, in condemning their theology, simply dismiss the life they exemplified and taught, for their works of discipline grew out of a desire to separate themselves from a world that knew nothing of the word "no." They did what they did for a reason. They had their sights on God. Their teachings were not for everybody then, and they won't be for everybody now. But their example is good for us to see.

It is written of Abba Dioscorus of Namisias: "Every year he made one particular resolution: not to meet anyone for a year, or not to speak, or not to taste cooked food, or not to eat any fruit. . . . This was his system in everything. He made himself master of one thing, and then started on another, and so on each year."

"Why?" some will ask. "To what end is all this?" ask others. But think about it. The man didn't have to do it; he did it for his own gain, and he did it for spiritual reasons too. When a person fights temptation, even innocent ones such as desiring a piece of cooked meat, he discovers that he has within him the ability to resist something far bigger. And before anyone discounts the value of this desire for obedience to the disciplined life by these early monks, before anyone scoffs, let that person ask, "Will I also scoff at Scripture?" For even if we refuse to learn from these monks, there are still the words of Jesus: "And take heed to yourselves, lest at any time your hearts be overcharged with surfeiting, and drunkenness, and cares of this life, and so that day come upon you unawares. For as a snare shall it come on all them that dwell on the face of the whole earth. Watch ye therefore, and pray always, that ye may be accounted worthy to escape all these things that shall come to pass, and to stand before the Son of man" (Luke 21:34–36, KJV).

Jesus told his disciples, "Whosoever will lose his life for my sake shall find it. For what is a man profited, if he shall gain the whole world, and lose his own soul? or what shall a man give in exchange for his soul?" (Matthew 16:25, 26, KJV).

Abba Cyrus of Alexandria said, "If you are not tempted, you have no hope: if you are not tempted, it is because you are used to sinning. The man who does not fight sin at the stage of temptation, sins in his body. And the man who sins in his body has no trouble from temptation."

What a far distance many of us are from Abba Evagrius who said, "Cut out of your heart the desire for many things, and so prevent the mind being disturbed, and the quiet wasted."

There is health in this "cutting-out" process. It is the discipline of not having, not grasping, not seeking personal pleasure, but rather holding to and loving God for who he is in himself. There is true worship in that because it is a worship that centers on him, not

70

self. It is a worship that God honors.

Yet too many of us simply allow ourselves to do what gives us pleasure; we have no controls, we leak out at the edges. Such an undisciplined life leads to all kinds of spiritual distress, and then we wonder why this distress has come. For many, even praying is undisciplined and hollow. I am still surprised, even though I've experienced it often, to meet Christian people, even pastors and church workers, who do not have a regular, disciplined time alone with God. When temptation comes, or problems emerge, they wonder what is wrong. They don't understand why they are so weak.

Many ignore the day-by-day meeting with God because, caught up as they are in the quest for spiritual thrills, they expect pleasure even from this prayer time too. And if pleasure with God (by their own definition of it) doesn't come, they stop having their time of personal worship.

For the sake of our pleasure, God has to titillate our senses to prove to us that he is near. If he doesn't, we go looking for something else. We have to hear voices, or have prickly feelings, or feel a warm glow. To many people that is all God is good for. As a result, for some people even the Christian life is an unhappy life because it is centered on the person who is taking, not on the holy God himself.

The riches of the Spirit-filled life don't just drop from heaven. God meets us in the discipline of daily obedience, and in it we are blessed in him. He meets us on his terms, not ours. His coming and his giving are his. If our human weakness has demanded certain experiences and signs, it is time for us to realize that if God were ruled by our spiritual lusts he would be no

71

God, he would be only the creation of our inner urgings. Scripture tells us: "We have this treasure in earthen vessels, that the excellency of the power may be of God, and not of us" (2 Corinthians 4:7, KJV).

In those early monasteries the younger monks watched and learned from the older ones. Even people who never entered the full monastic orders came to spend a year or two with these brothers—not just to secure their salvation, as many of us have tended to assume, but to learn what the Apostle Paul taught, to work out their own salvation with fear and trembling. (See Philippians 2:12, KJV.)

We had better be learners of obedience and discipline too. Speaking in Scripture, Wisdom says, "Blessed is the man who listens to me, watching daily at my gates, waiting at my doorposts. For he who finds me finds life, and obtains favor from the Lord. But he who sins against me injures himself" (Proverbs 8:34–36, NASB).

The old monastics were stable. They were part of the church, giving their lives to it. They were under its umbrella. Today's "monastics" are too. These Christians do not spend their time sniffing the wind for the latest theological fad to chase, or for the teachings of a celebrity to follow. They do not shop around for a more exciting preacher or for the titillating, vicarious thrills that come from hearing about the former sinful life of the newest Christian superstar. They are not spiritual gadflies, unwilling to make a commitment unless there is some personal thrill or recognition in it. Theirs is not a cafeteria religion, sampling a little of this and a little of that, taking whatever appeals to the spiritual palate at the moment. These are not sideshow frequenters who tour the Christian midway, listening to this barker or that one calling to "come see what we have here."

The "new monastics" (and this is a good term to apply to disciplined believers) are willing to do today what those monastics did in the context of their earlier centuries. For although time and events change, the basic commitment of the believer is the same.

Disciplined believers labor for the fellowship. They pray, they teach, they love, they nurture. They have a purpose in their devotion and they practice it day in and day out. They go without, not out of spiritual pride but because they do not have spiritual pride. They want to yield to God.

Discipline is not just following rules, nor is it even copying the early monks; it is existing in and for the One who owns us. We practice discipline neither for self-conceit nor to brag about it, but for him. We obey God because it is the moral and right thing to do.

Committed, disciplined Christians trust God and go on with him every day no matter what the circumstances of their lives. They do so because they must. They know from experience and reason that there is no other way to go. The One who said, "I will never leave thee, nor forsake thee" (Hebrews 13:5, KJV), has always kept his word. We can live within the security of that assurance.

Those early disciplined monastics did the difficult thing and did it for God. They lived in a world that lacked discipline, and we do too. They were proof to themselves that man can serve God first. They worked at it—they learned to say no.

They knew something that William Law also knew. In his book, *A Serious Call to a Devout and Holy*

*Life,* he said, "If religion commands us to live wholly unto God, and to do all to His glory, it is because every other way is living wholly against ourselves, and will end in our own shame and confusion of face."

We have moved a long way from that; we have moved too far. It is time to find again what the monastics had. We must come not to a form of monasticism that is nonevangelical and ingrown, shut off from the world with only occasional excursions out to it, but rather a monasticism in which we are shut in with Christ and at the same time shut in with the world.

Is this contrary to reality? Is this a movement against ourselves? No, it isn't. We are not living against ourselves when we follow him. It is "ourselves" that interests him. All that we have read and heard about "me" and "my pleasures" and "my development" and "myself" is what God wants for me too. But he is the giver, the Source, not I. He alone knows the "me" part of myself.

We are false to true self when we seek for ourselves and are not yielded to the One who alone can provide what we need and want. James McConkey said, "To walk in the Spirit—not to walk in the flesh—is the whole secret of the believer's life of power, privilege and peace. But for the believer to walk in the Spirit, the first essential is his absolute yielding to God of all control and direction of his life."

Try something. Find the command of God that is hardest for you to obey. Then commit your obedience to God and practice living that commandment as if that commandment were no longer being broken by you. You will find that when we give something to God and practice it, we do succeed. He takes away the desire to renege on our promise.

There are thousands of Christians who have experienced deliverance from something that has kept them from a life of obedience because they finally identified their need, took upon themselves the obligation of praying about it, and then did what they promised God they would do. God has reinforced their promise with results. Followers of Jesus do not practice obedience to become someone, but they practice obedience because they *are* someone—God's person. And they intend to leave behind anything and everything that keeps them from being fit representatives of all that is holy.

There is liberty in saying no because it moves us out of the narrow inlet blocked by debris into the great open ocean of the yesses of God. "Yes" turns us from the shallow, from the weak, the restrictive, to the deep, the strong, the liberating—to the resources of the Omnipotent God. He is the One who has a dream for us. He is the One who puts everything together in a magnificent yes. And for us, to be there with him in his great yes, is the happiest state of all! Richard Foster (*The Celebration of Discipline*) is right, and he answers the millions who do not know what they are rejecting when he says, "When one's inner spirit is free from all that holds it down, that can hardly be described as dull drudgery."

What in fact holds us down is what the unknowing world calls "liberty." That liberty is no liberty at all. Speak of liberty and freedom and excitement to the one who has practiced sexual promiscuity and is en-

slaved by it. He doesn't have liberty at all. A student
newspaper on the campus of Cambridge University
in England printed this story:

> Two girl students at Cambridge University bet
> on who could go to bed with the most men in
> five days.
> The staggering score for the blue-stocking sex
> orgy was 98-62.
> Another brainy bird at the revered seat of
> learning boasted that she would have sex with
> every man in her college . . . all 400 of them.

Are they free?

Speak of liberty and joy and freedom to one in-
fected by venereal disease.

Speak of liberty to the mother who had her child
murdered in the womb and now has to live with that
thought until the day she dies.

Talk of liberty to one who is so controlled by the
need to succeed, to have power, prestige, or riches
that he is unable to give his heart, his life, his resources, or his skills to anything else. He may as well
be in prison.

Cry "liberty" to the one who has no self-control,
who is unable to withstand anything, who is plea-
sure-oriented, who has missed his calling, whose gifts
lie untouched, whose love is strapped and unex-
pressed, whose power is gone.

Tell these people that they are free. To do that is to
whistle in the dark, for we know that it is not true.
Worse, they know it too.

Thomas Merton said, "In Christ there is no conflict
and no anguish, no dissension and no shadow of divi-

sion, no change, no sorrow. . . . In Him we find
both liberty and security."

It is never too late to say no. The freedom offered
in Christ is that we can say no, and when we say it
there comes the opposite resounding yes. And out of
that yes God builds a life more beautiful, more complete, more satisfying than anything that we could
ever create for ourselves. He wants that for each of us.

For over ten years, first on an eastern campus and
then in the midwest, I ministered to university students. We would meet regularly to pray for each
other. Sometimes, in small groups, we would ask
each other, "How can I pray for you to be the obedient man or woman God wants you to be? What are
the blocks that need to be eliminated, what are the
changes that need to be made?" And as we prayed
specifically for obedience and holiness and faith, I
could see God take those young lives and develop
them.

I see how he has honored those times of serious
prayer. Wherever I go now, I meet these students
with whom I once prayed or who prayed for me, and
I see what God is doing in their lives. I compare them
to others who missed that time of praying because
they were not willing to let God have them—to be all
that God wanted them to be—and I see the difference.

A. H. McNeile said: "A man's soul grows, if it is
growing, like his body, with a slow imperceptible
motion, as a result of everything that he does, every
breath that he breathes, and everything that he eats
and drinks." God offers this to us. He is our life; he is
our gain.

# SIX
# My Life, My Gain

† *But know that the Lord hath set apart him that is godly for himself* [Psalm 4:3, KJV].

We have to be honest. Each of us will ask the question, "What's in this for me?"

We'll ask because we are selfish. It is human to be so. It would be a lie to deny that.

One evening in March 1955, I sat in the home of a certified public accountant. We were not discussing money. He was talking to me about Jesus Christ. Through the Scriptures he showed me what salvation means. It was the first time that anyone had ever done that for me.

I listened, but I argued too. I was a college freshman—fairly smart, I thought—and having argued religion before with my friends and having read a little about religion, I had my own beliefs about it.

I had usually done quite well in the past with the argument: "That's fine for you. *I* don't need it." Or, when people really got pushy: "Religion is a weak man's crutch." And then there was the one I used that usually made religious people fold: "I'm as good as any of those hypocrites in the church."

But this man didn't argue with me or react defensively to my rehearsed lines. He simply opened his Bible, placed it on a coffeetable in front of us, and pointed to what it said. He responded to my remarks with, "Look what the Bible says." And as he did this, he was wise enough not to flip from book to book or try to impress me with all that he had learned. He stayed in one book, Paul's letter to the Romans, and always he let me read it for myself. That night I became a Christian. Since then I've never doubted the power that is in the Word of God.

My CPA friend started with Romans 3:23: "For all have sinned, and come short of the glory of God" (Romans 3:23, KJV). It's good that he did because I had no real trouble with that verse. There was no difficulty in my mind about believing that all people are sinful; I could see that by observing people around me and by looking at myself. I learned later how defensive some Christians become about "sin," even just the word, as if they have to explain or justify biblical statements about it. They don't. Most of the people I knew who did not believe in Christ had no problem believing in sin. Most honest people admit that if there is a God, they don't measure up to his standards. What sustains them, and particularly what keeps them from coming to Christ, is not unbelief about sin but their belief in "justice." Just about everyone believes that he is not as bad as the next person. People range in their self-justification from "I suppose that I'll make it" to "I'm no criminal."

I could accept Romans 3:23. It was a straight-out statement and I agreed with it. I suppose anyone who looks squarely at himself will admit that. The ones who won't acknowledge sin are dodging publicly what they know to be true. But they admit it, most of them, in the privacy of their own minds.

Then my CPA friend turned a few pages in his Bible to Romans 6:23, and that's when I began to argue. The verse states, "For the wages of sin is death; but the gift of God is eternal life through Jesus Christ our Lord" (Romans, 6:23, KJV). I did what most people do when they see that Scripture; I trotted out the argument, "How can a just God condemn anybody to hell? How can God, if he is a God of love, not take everybody to heaven?" Having used that argument or some variation of it before, I knew that it usually made Christians stutter. This time it didn't work.

"Read it again," he said. When I had, he asked me, "What are wages?" Well, that's not hard to answer when you have a job, and I did. I punched a time clock, rolled up my sleeves, and worked. So he asked me, "When you receive your paycheck every two weeks, is that a gift?" The answer was so obvious it was silly. Of course the paycheck was not a gift; I earned the money! "Then," he said, "you would never say that when your employer gives you your paycheck he is giving you a gift."

"Right," I agreed.

He emphasized, "The wages of sin is death. The sinner is working too; he is working at his sin and he will earn his wages. He works for it, he earns it, and he will receive it. It is his own doing. God does not condemn him to hell. He chooses to work toward it. He can work a little or he can work a lot, but his "time card" doesn't have God's name on it, nor does he receive God's wages. He receives the wages he is working for."

I had nothing to say. My friend went on. "But," he pointed out, and stressed that something opposite usually follows the "but" in Scripture, "the gift of God is eternal life through Jesus Christ our Lord."

"Now," he asked, "what are you doing to earn that gift?"

I answered, "If you earn a gift, it's not a gift. The only way to receive a gift is to simply put out your hand and take it."

"Well," he said, "God is offering you a gift. Why don't you take it?"

Then I argued some more, but this time not from my "logic" but from my emotions. "This is too simple. There has to be a catch," I said. So he repeated the verse again.

I thought a long time about that, and I'm not sure if it was a head response or a feeling response, but I knew that the Bible made sense. Then he turned to another passage in the same book. This time it was Romans 10:9, 10: "If thou shalt confess with thy mouth the Lord Jesus, and shalt believe in thine heart that God hath raised him from the dead, thou shalt be saved. For with the heart man believeth unto righteousness; and with the mouth confession is made unto salvation."

"Anyone can say he believes," I argued. "Is that all you want me to do? Okay," I said sarcastically, "I believe."

He wasn't offended.

"There's more, isn't there? It says, 'Believe in your heart that God raised him from the dead.' The sacrifice of Jesus is not only that he died," he said. "The work of Jesus not only involved his death but his resurrection. He overcame the power of death. The life that he offers now, eternal life, is a resurrected life, a life after the grave. That's what he offers you—not life that is only a before-death life but life forever from this point on—eternal life."

I believed that, but believing it didn't mean that I was ready to confess that I believed it and I sneered about those people who readily confess Jesus. "I've seen those 'Christians,'" I said.

But Scripture won because Scripture is clear and is truth. A response to God is in both the believing and the confessing, not just one or the other. A person believes and confesses—and so he is saved. I knew I had to do *something*.

Then he put the question to me: "If you want that gift of life, what is stopping you from receiving it now?"

I admitted that there was nothing stopping me except my own fear of the unknown. I knew where I was; I didn't know where believing in Jesus would take me.

He prayed for me then, and I said yes to Christ. It was so simple and unemotional that the only reason I remember it is that I knew then and know now that I did indeed receive new life that night. It was a "birth day." All my living dates from that night.

Then he showed me one more passage of Scripture, Romans 8:1: "There is therefore now no condemnation to them which are in Christ Jesus." None! No longer condemned—that meant me! And although it took days, maybe weeks, for that to settle into my awareness, those words "no condemnation" set me free.

Most of what I had done that Thursday night, March 10, 1955, was not fully clear to me then. The act of transferring my trust from myself to Jesus Christ was probably not an act of devotion. I can't even say that I received Jesus as my Savior because I loved Jesus. Later, as I came to understand more fully what he did for me in the incarnation, the crucifixion, the resurrection, I came to love him very much. But not then. I didn't know enough then. Rather I responded to Christ that night because his atonement made sense to me. I did not want to be separated from God for all eternity— I did not want to be lost by my own choice. I wanted heaven; I did not want hell. And I am quite certain that there is no other way to explain my initial response to Jesus other than "selfishness." I wanted God on my side. I wanted to belong to him. For me it was a "selfish" act.

Now, years later, I can exclaim, as James McConkey does, "Jesus: Savior! How much the word means! He has saved us from the guilt of sin. He is saving us from the power of sin. He will save us from the presence of sin."

I have learned that God is at work in me, "both to will and to do of his good pleasure" (Philippians 2:13, KJV). Those words are true. I can and do live in peace knowing that he is thinking of me constantly (Psalm 139:17, 18, TLB). I rejoice in the gifts he chooses to use, knowing that I am fearfully and wonderfully made (Psalm 139:14, KJV). But I could not say all of that on that March night in 1955. My entrance into life in Christ was based on rebirth; the gains of my new life came later.

There is nothing wrong with starting like that. "What's in this for me?" is a legitimate question. "How is this going to help me?"

It is not wrong to be selfish like that. Selfishness is the starting point. Selfishness made me want redemption. Because God made me for himself, he desires me. I needed to know that.

It was for eternal life, and to have a reason for living now, that I came to him. Adoration came later.

It was for my life and my gain that God asked me to surrender to him. James McConkey says, "And what is this act of surrender? It is the yielding of the life to God to do and suffer all His will in all things and in all times, because we have, once for all, settled that it is the best thing for us." To yield to Christ was the best thing for me to do.

Jesus Christ is for me. He has declared me to be priceless in value—he has proved it. Christ is the measure of my worth, for he is the price paid for me. Sometimes when I try to help someone to see the value God places on a human soul, I'll ask him that question: "What has he paid for you?" The answer, of course, is that he paid Jesus. And my reply: "Then, when you can tell me what Jesus Christ is worth to God the Father, I'll tell you what you are worth to God the Father because the price he paid for your redemption is his Son Jesus Christ."

I am of value to God; I am adopted into his family (Romans 8:14–17). I see that and I do not deny it. He has given me life. He has redeemed my soul. He wants me to have the gains of this soul-redeemed life. He does not want me to exhaust my energies trying to become something on my own terms, for my sights are not as high as his. Rather, he is shaping my life and using my life as he cares to, as I surrender it to him for his fulfillment and completion.

And in my "selfishness" I want to be all that he designed me to be, all that he saved me to be. In the development of the gifts that he has placed in me, how foolish if I only follow after others, trying to be like them, a carbon copy of someone else, and miss the fulfillment that he has for me. I come to the recognition that I am an original because he made me so.

In this Christ-original life, I don't fret nearly as much as I used to about what comes or what doesn't come, or worry about the days left to me. I have adequate time to become what he wants me to be, enough time to live. If I die at an early age, that is no loss. There is no incomplete work, assuming that my day-by-day desire has been to seek him, to serve him, and to allow him to work his will in me. If my time is not mine, and it isn't, then there is no such thing as "early" death or "unfinished" work. What matters is that I keep on going with him, either now in the body or then in spirit. No matter which, I continue with him, in his plan, under his control, moving either through time or into eternity. It is all the same with him—and me. If I am taken in the midst of my days of productive work or witness, that is no loss—that is gain. He is God. I'll worship him now in faith and later face to face.

When my friend Paul Little died in an automobile crash in Canada, I was in Stockholm, Sweden, and did not immediately hear the news. A few days after his death, my wife Andrea joined me in London. We were going on to Keswick together. Wisely, she waited until we had left Heathrow Airport and were on a bus before she leaned over to tell me the news of Paul's death. Then she let me handle the shock while she looked out the window.

I said what I suppose everybody else said at that time: "Why?" "Why, God, when he was doing so much for you and his most fruitful days still seemed to be ahead. Why?" There was no explanation then and there isn't an explanation now, except that it was God's time, and Paul Little was always serving on God's time.

Our work is never our work; it is his, and we are to be faithful with the days that we have, just as Jesus himself was faithful, though his earthly work was, by human definition, never "finished." More people were sick who could have been healed, more were hungry who could have been fed, more were confused who could have been taught. But his time of incarnation was finished at his death. His redemptive work was in his dying, in his resurrection; and it continues now through the work of the Holy Spirit in his Church. His work goes on, for he said, "If I go not away, the Comforter will not come unto you; but if I depart, I will send him unto you. And when he is come, he will reprove the world of sin, and of righteousness, and of judgment: Of sin, because they believe not on me; of righteousness, because I go to my Father, and ye see me no more; of judgment, because the prince of this world is judged" (John 16:7–11, KJV).

The follower of Jesus belongs to an eternal plan. It is God's work that he does and God's greater life that he lives, whether it is here with him today or home with him tomorrow. "Ye are not your own. For ye are bought with a price" (1 Corinthians 6:19, 20, KJV).

"I am," declared the Apostle Paul, "crucified with Christ: nevertheless I live; yet not I, but Christ liveth in me: and the life which I now live in the flesh I live by the faith of the Son of God, who loved me, and gave himself for me" (Galatians 2:20, KJV).

In this life we don't have to waste our time fretting about where we fit in. God knows where we fit in. Nor are we to worry about the value of various segments of our time; God knows that too. He did not make me to be like someone else or to follow someone else's pattern. I am uniquely, fearfully, and wonderfully made; known before I was born. And that is the most liberating knowledge that anyone can have.

We are not in the process of expanding our consciousness to be like him, as some teach. But because we are in him and he is abiding in us, we *do* expand. We expand because he is expanding us. It is our fitting nature to be in him, and for his life to be in us. We are misfits if this is not so. Three times in John 15:4 we read the word *abide*. "Abide in me, and I in you. As the branch cannot bear fruit of itself, except it abide in the vine; no more can ye, except ye abide in me" (John 15:4, KJV).

That's what life in Christ is all about—abiding. It is not the fruit-producing that matters, it is the abiding. The producing comes from the vine; the branches are only the fruit bearers. To be an abiding branch is to be a faithful branch. The fruit will come. And the fruit that is borne, whether it be large fruit or small, abundant or not so abundant, is his doing. Our role is to be attached to the vine, to fit into our place—to abide.

Union with him, that's what counts. Out of that union comes the gain. It is gain as he designs it and causes it, and a gain that we can enjoy because the enjoyment is part of the belonging. The security of it, the peace of it, and the results of it are for us.

Struggle is no longer there when we abide. For no longer are we somehow trying to lift ourselves toward him, or trying to be perfect in him, or attempting somehow to hold down our independent wills for him; we do not practice our own style of obedience. Obedience is a coming together with him in confidence and trust. This eliminates tension, anxiety, and, in fact, eliminates all the torment that grips so many "unattached" people.

To struggle always in tension with God, to be up and down endlessly like a teeter-totter—never going anywhere yet always being in motion—is such a foolish waste of existence. Trying to please him and yet at the same time trying to please self is just the opposite of what he wants and blesses. No wonder so many people go through new crises in their twenties and thirties and forties. Every change in life is traumatic when a person goes through it on his own.

We are not to be always trying to fit everything together with God as if we could by our poor effort cement a relationship with the Eternal. God wants us to belong to him; then everything fits together. Then each event in life begins to have purpose.

It's not important to understand fully God's purposes. The Father knows. And in Jesus Christ we know the Father. We don't always have to convince ourselves that all is well or that we are successful, or use any of the other so-called measures that others use; God has told us that he is in control, and he is. The good that God determines is going to be worked out whether or not we understand it (Romans 8:28). He will be God. Where we are going in relationship to him is a decision we do not have to make or even know. Never is it "what will I do?" in order to be in God's will, in order to receive the gains in life that come from him. Rather, the question is, "What will my relationship be with God?"

God alone defines life for us because he is life. Our duty is not to perform a spiritual balancing act, to fit God into our lives or our lives into God. Ours is not an attempt to find wholeness and purpose within the confusion of life. Our responsibility is to be in him. This is the will of God for us. In this he is glorified; in this we live out our praise.

Thomas Kelly, in his *Testament of Devotion,* said, "He is the center and source of action, not the end point of thought." God is not someone we try to find; he is the very Center of our being and we act within that Center. Again, it was Kelly who said, "The strong man must become the little child, not understanding but trusting the Father. . . .

"They have found the secret of the Nazarene, and, not content to assent to it intellectually, they have committed to it in action, and walk in newness of life in the vast fellowship of unceasing prayer."

"Yes, I am his," is not something we say with our fingers crossed. It is a walk, a stepping-out in the awareness that we are his for him to watch and develop in a life that is meaningful, whether or not it is "successful" by man's standards.

Whether life is rewarding in human terms means nothing; "rewarding" as a measure of life is nonsense. For in ever deeper ways with God we are brought into an exciting frontier of spiritual life that moves forward with a sense of wholeness and with an anticipation (not wishful thinking but secure awareness), that even more is coming in the future because every day we are growing in him and in our capacity to enjoy him.

God has me! That's an affirmation based on reality: the reality of his promise, the reality of his character, the reality of his action, the reality of his own reputation. Therefore, whereas we can never have happiness or security so long as we are struggling to belong to him, we can have it quickly by accepting his offers. So long as we are always trying to have some kind of oneness with him, a struggle from our part toward God, we will not find that fulfillment. Nor will it come until we admit that we are building on man's efforts and stop doing it. He wants that oneness with us; we must yield ourselves to it.

This doesn't mean we should abandon reason. Nor does it mean we should meekly surrender because we are tired and can no longer battle. Nor are we asked to deny the Scripture "work out your own salvation with fear and trembling" (Philippians 2:12, KJV), for that verse is based on a relationship that already exists, built on salvation in Christ on his terms, in his way (Philippians 2:13). This is a completing process that God has designed from the beginning. It comes from that divine union. The self is fulfilled by the God who made that self, gave that self, redeemed that self, and now fills that self and uses it.

In my life I have no limits because God who owns me has no limits. If any limits do come in, they are self-imposed. They are imposed by me when I try to determine what God can and cannot do in my life, always measuring him by my own human understanding of God—a measure based on me, the one created; not on him, the Creator. He understands who I am and what he wants to fulfill in me. He knows how he wants to answer my prayers. He knows how he wants to use this life that he has designed.

If he didn't, he never would have designed me and

created me in the first place. God had a reason for me, and if I will accept that, then I can begin to live. With A. W. Tozer I can say, "My God, I shall not waste time deploring my weakness or my unfittedness for the work. The responsibility is not mine, but thine. Thou hast said, 'I knew thee—ordained thee—I sanctified thee,' and thou hast also said, 'Thou shalt go to all to whom I shall send thee, and whatsoever I command thee thou shalt speak.' Who am I to argue with thee or to call into question thy sovereign choice? The decision is not mine, but thine. So be it, Lord. Thy will, not mine, be done."

Self-esteem? Yes! He gives self-esteem and will give a better life through that self-esteem. You will begin to discover as he shapes your life that at last you have something more to offer to God and something more to offer other people. Our lives gain because we are offering our lives to him who is life itself. To keep back parts of our lives is not self-control but theft. As we keep, we lose; as we give, we gain. Jesus said that "whosoever will save his life shall lose it: and whosoever will lose his life for my sake shall find it" (Matthew 16:25, KJV). He meant what he said then; he means it now.

I am and have a precious self; God made that self and gave me that self. It is my life. I can rejoice in it because God is so much and, as a result of being his, I have so much.

This is not a state of passive behavior; this is an exciting, active behavior. This is a self-realization by and through his revelation. Unlike people who behave as experimental rats in a laboratory, able to take only so many shocks before they quit and won't struggle any more, we can go on and live and expand no matter what shocks come. God gives us hope for going on and a reason for doing so. This is the opposite to helplessness, the opposite to hopelessness. This is the excitement that there is no end to growth and fulfillment while we are here on earth, and no end when we depart from this life.

In Christ I am free to live, free to be flexible, free to move, free to fail, free to succeed. I can confidently know that there are things I will do well and things that I will not be able to do at all. I don't have to try to prove to myself or to others that somehow I can be what I am not. God made me; God owns me.

And as I relax in Christ, I begin to see that there have always been people like me. This reinforces my certainty. I meet people in Scripture—people like Abraham, Moses, Stephen—who did not fully understand themselves or their purpose, but they knew that God understood them. They did not always feel strong or healthy or wise. They wondered at God's commands as sometimes I do. Even the disciple who loved Jesus most didn't always understand everything he did or taught. Realizing this allows me to have moments of depression; it allows me to cry and pound my fists on God's chest. It allows me to be the person I am because I am God's person. I can look to my Creator because I am his. I can look to my Redeemer; I can look ahead to fulfillment and to deliverance. And I can be happy even in my "failures," waiting to see how these too will be used because I am secure in the One who made me and owns me.

I know that there is a tomorrow. I understand with David that my mistakes do not end my usefulness for all time. I know with Peter that even denial is not permanent. I see and know and believe with the

Apostle Paul that even "if we believe not, yet he abideth faithful: he cannot deny himself" (2 Timothy 2:13, KJV).

It took me a long time to learn that. I have not always understood the dark nights of my crying when God was drawing me away from the things that might control me. I have not always understood when I have resisted him that I was tugging and pulling against God, seeking for myself what was less than his best.

I have not always been able to "count it all joy" with James and see pain as part of the building process. I have not always understood that God is looking at me—always (1 Samuel 16:7). In depression or the physical disorders brought on by emotional turmoil, I have not always recognized my own anger or my fighting with God.

And when I've run into a dead end, I've not always understood that it was a prelude to a new beginning. I still do not always see this, but I'm learning.

It takes some people a long time to learn that God will not hurt them. Martin Luther knew that. In a letter to a friend he said, "I am sorry to hear that you are still depressed at times. Christ is as near to you as you are to yourself, and he will not harm you, for he shed his blood for you. . . . Believe that he esteems and loves you more than does Dr. Luther or any other Christian."

I've experienced that; I know the love of Christians because I know the love of Christ. Their tears, their embrace, their tenderness, their edification and correction, have been mine. The love of his Church is for me a touch of his love, the human channel through which the love of God flows. He has always tried to tell me, "I love you"; I realize that now.

I know that God is seeking to give me more of himself. He is, as Thomas Kelly put it, "Anxious to swell out our time-nows into an Eternal Now by filling them with a sense of Presence."

I can see him as the active one in my life—regardless of what I call good or bad—I see the gains he wants me to make and how he works those out day by day. I can understand now that saintliness and holiness come from growing in him.

William Law in his *Serious Call to a Devout and Holy Life* said, "Would you know who is the greatest saint in the world: it is not he who prays most or fasts most; it is not he who gives most alms, or is most eminent for temperance, chastity, or justice; but it is he who is always thankful to God, who wills everything that God willeth, who receives every thing as an instance of God's goodness, and has a heart always ready to praise God for it." Then he went on to say, "A life thus devoted unto God, looking wholly unto Him in all our actions, and doing all things suitably to His glory is so far from being dull and uncomfortable, that it creates new comforts in every thing that we do."

Knowing this is both the fulfillment to life and the doorway to a still greater expansion of my being. To sense the love and the completion and the gain that God builds into life is to live indeed!

If we could only communicate this to others, they could be fulfilled too. How obviously empty, then, would be that secular seeking of God on "my terms in my way." How foolish would be the competition of person with person as if a success measure was all that counted—certainly Christians would no longer do it.

God wants to satisfy, to enlarge, to offer; there is so much more of his grace to be had. When we gain some of it, then we can claim still more for there are so many more of his promises to claim, so much more of himself to have. And as we do claim him, we will know all the more clearly that we are his friends, no matter what, no matter where. And we will follow him, regardless.

# SEVEN
# Regardless

† *Put on the new self, created to be like God in true righteousness and holiness* [Ephesians 4:24, NIV].

Malcolm Smith tells the story of a man on a business trip who found that his host company's hospitality included a girl for his pleasure. He almost succumbed. Driving her to his hotel, he started struggling with the seventh commandment. He drove her home, went back to his hotel, and fell on his knees crying. Smith wrote, "He began to force his words out in prayer. 'Oh, God, if only I had taken that girl back because I loved You. But I took her back because I was afraid of You. I was just terrified of the consequences. God, I don't love You. I don't know You.' He choked on, ashamed and stung at having to have made the statement at all."

Most of us have come to realize that we will always struggle like that; we will always wonder about our commitment to God. In one sense it helps to know that this is the way it will be because then we can say, "Please, God, help me!" And with a determination that is an abandonment to Christ, we can stumble after him with our promise, "I am going to be an imitator of God, regardless" (Ephesians 5:1, NIV).

"I am going to learn Christ, regardless" (Ephesians 4:20, KJV).

"I will follow him and obey, regardless!"

But if any of us continues to seek only "happiness," as those people who have no Christ, that kind of commitment will never be made. Knowing about Christ and being in Christ are not the same. Knowing about him is not attachment to him. Short of a vine-and-branches relationship, no experience with religion, even with institutionalized Christianity, will keep us from succumbing to the ownership of our environment which is influenced by what is called in the Bible "the spirit who is now at work in those who are disobedient" (Ephesians 2:2, NIV).

Some may say, "I will try to be attached to Jesus. I will try to be like him; I will try to obey." They become frustrated, unhappy, and have more problems than ever because they are trying to be something that they are not. Only the branches, because they are attached, can relax and be. They belong. For to be attached to Jesus Christ as the branch is attached to the vine is a natural way to live. There is no effort to it. The branch doesn't "try to hang on" when the storms come. It belongs. Its life is not something it has to work out for itself; it is part of the vine. It doesn't have to struggle to produce "and do great things for the vine"; it just has to be. Its relationship will take care of the fruit-bearing. It has a relationship that is right, natural, and easy.

But, like the ancient Greeks, too many of us have come to look at faith, life, and holiness as an ideal rather than a practice. We have religion and we have life. And, carefully, we keep them separate. We carry with us through life the very things that cannot be part of true worship: our idols, our other gods.

But when we choose to be abandoned to Christ, to serve him and not mammon, then we will be no longer divided in our thinking, and, most important, we will not want to be. Regardless of any other consideration, we will be obedient to God as best we understand his leading, his teaching, and his purpose for us. We will obey him—regardless.

When I make that promise to him, then no longer can I allow Satan to use my wants to destroy me. Regardless of where a commitment leads I will faithfully obey the One who is above all and in all and through all—not for my sake but for his sake. When I look at my accomplishments, I will do so in the light of who he is, and will even try to see my suffering as he sees it. I will learn to see my development and growth not just in terms of the immediate but in the larger dimension of the eternal. No more will I struggle with temptation just to overcome it, but moving beyond that I will seek to overcome temptation in order to love him and serve him for his sake.

I will picture holiness and focus on it, following him regardless, being good because he owns me. It will be more than acts done; it will be a way of life based on ownership and the living out of that owned life. And, if this commitment seems strange to professing Christians, it only proves how far so many of us have strayed from true obedience and faith.

Others know that half-hearted obedience is a contradiction. For even from Islam, which Christians call less than truth, have come such teachings: "Surrendering one's entire life to the will of Allah is the keystone of the Islamic faith. For the Muslim faithful, Allah is in all things."

"Islam is not a part of life, it is a way of life," said associate professor Iraj Bashiri, an Iranian native who teaches Iranian studies at the University of Minnesota. "It is woven," he said, "into the very fabric of life."

Can it be less so for us who name the name of Jesus Christ?

We don't know fully, nor can we know, the results of obedience to him or where that obedience may lead; we only know that step by step each day we are to obey God prayerfully—we must do it, regardless. As Dietrich Bonhoeffer explained, "Only Jesus Christ, who bids us follow him, knows the journey's end."

When Jesus called Peter, his first words to that fisherman were, "Follow me" (Mark 1:17). And at the end of the gospels (John 21:22), those were also the last recorded words that Jesus spoke to him—"Follow me."

As disciples, our obedience to Christ lies between those two calls. We begin our Christian life by obeying the command, "Follow me." All life long we hear, "Follow me." And at the end of our life we hear it again, "Follow me"—right on into eternity.

The question to ask is not, "Will such a commitment to follow Jesus regardless really work?" The question is, "Will I make that commitment?"

What is stopping you from making such a commitment now? Is it fear? Think about the fears that rule you, the ones that control your life, the fear that you think must be met on your terms in your way. What fear could possibly be stronger than his power, his blessing and his love in ownership of you? What fear would control you and keep you from true liberty in Christ?

Is it a fear of the loss of your health? Are you asking, "What if I get sick? What if I can no longer work? What if I lose my eyes or my legs?" Or are you saying, "I need to stay with a company with a good health insurance plan. I can't break away to do what I think God is calling me to do." There are people living like that. Are you one of them? They are fearful, they are owned, they are unable to live free lives in Christ.

Is it the fear of some financial failure? "What if I get too far into debt? What if my house depreciates because of a highway coming through or the construction of a nuclear power plant? What if my stock values plunge? What if I lose my savings through inflation or a strike?"

Is it job security? "Will I be replaced by a younger person, a better educated person, a machine? What if the company folds or they phase out my department? Will I get my vested interest in the pension plan?"

Is it the loss of social position? "What if I can't maintain my club memberships? Will I be elected president of my organization? Will I be able to reciprocate the invitations I receive? What if I stop receiving those invitations? I need important people around me, and others know people who are more important than the ones I know. What if my spouse embarrasses me? What if I can't attain the goals and prominence I've always dreamed about?"

Is it an identity crisis? "I thought by this time in my life I would know who I am. I still don't know where I am going or why I'm here. Why does this have to happen to me? I'm tired of struggling to be something when I don't know who I am. I thought my problems would be solved by now, but middle age and success have only brought different problems."

Those fears will own you. You will serve them.

The way to be free is to face those fears and see them for what they are—temptations. Then place those fears against what you have in Christ.

What's the worst thing that can happen to you? Sickness? Death? You are already dead in Christ, so all is gain. As one Christian put it, that's what we are all getting ready for—the translation, to be with him. Why are we afraid as if we have nothing to look forward to?

You ask, "What if I lose everything I have, my financial security?" Well, what did you have when you came into this world? Most people who fear financial losses are the ones who already have more than most. They are not poor. They fear what will happen to them, when, in fact, if the worst did happen, they would be no worse off than other people in the world.

I remember wrestling with this when I was a seminary student. I wanted to resolve the question, "Am I prepared to go hungry?" I worked as a waiter in the seminary dining hall. It was one of my three jobs. Waiters were allowed to eat the meal they served. But there were more waiters than there were opportunities to work, and a night came when I had no money for food and was not scheduled to wait on tables. I was prepared to go hungry that night and committed my situation to God. Then a few minutes before dinner, a friend called and asked, "Would you be willing to wait tables for me tonight? It's my turn but I have a conflict." I did, and I ate. God could have let me go without, but he chose to arrange for me to eat. I'm ready to go hungry; that day may still come, but so far I've never had to go without a meal. If that comes, or anything else, there will come also the strength of God to match it.

Cameron Thompson in his book *Master Secrets of Prayer* said, "Rejoice if your needs are great, if they are ever mounting, if they are incredible, if they are impossible! The very trials God puts you through are to enlarge your heart so that He can bless you the more."

We worry about job security. Why? If we do that we are open to doing the unethical, the shady, even if it violates our consciences, in order to hold onto a job. But when we settle in our minds that we are prepared to do any kind of honest work, we are free. Best of all, as free beings, God can move us around as he wishes. Very often people stay with a company for years past the time when they realize they should be elsewhere just because there is security or the promise of a pension there. They are no longer available even to be led to something better. They are caught. People fear losing what in fact owns them. We only have one life, yet so many do nothing more with it than earn money.

Sometimes we put the need for social position or status above serving. Even Christians do that. They cannot do the commonplace or the ordinary; it is "beneath" them. It's even hard sometimes for Christians to ask their brothers and sisters to pray for them because they think they lose face when they admit that they have such a need for prayer. They feel that they are admitting to a weakness, an inability "to handle it on my own."

It works the other way, too. Sometimes Christians can't handle another Christian's legitimate opportunities. I remember once asking students, who were not impressed one way or the other by anything I did, to pray for a particular responsibility I had in Europe. I couldn't ask the church people to pray because several people had used the time for prayer requests only as a means of announcing their accomplishments. Prayer was a "brag" time. Instead of praying for a real need that I had, they would have seen my request as an announcement of the trip. So I said nothing to them. The students, on the other hand, were secure and free—free enough to pray for my ministry.

Who or what I am to others isn't a primary matter if I know what the Apostle Paul knew: "I am crucified with Christ: nevertheless I live; yet not I, but Christ liveth in me: and the life which I now live in the flesh I live by the faith of the Son of God, who loved me, and gave himself for me" (Galatians 2:20, KJV). I am his. I cannot know all that this means. I belong to him; that is freeing. I cannot grasp his mind on matters influencing me. I cannot know all that God knows about who I am and what I am to him.

Knowing God, knowing that he is in control of life, and being yielded to that control make a person live in harmony with him; he is one with God. That's what makes a whole human being. We may not recognize that very quickly because there are so many "unwhole" people around. We tend to look for the meaning of life among the majority, but they are not whole. They cannot give us a measure of the meaning of life because they don't have true life.

Dietrich Bonhoeffer explained: "With the loss of the Godlike nature God had given him, man had forfeited the destiny of his being, which was to be like God. In short, man had ceased to be man. He must live without the ability to live." We cannot judge the value of life by measuring against those who have never "passed from death unto life" (1 John 3:14, KJV). We can only judge the value of life against the true Lifegiver—Jesus Christ.

You've looked at your fears and doubts, the questions that keep you from letting go and living freely with the One who came to give you abundant life. Now look at his Word:

"And ye shall know the truth, and the truth shall make you free" (John 8:32, KJV).

"I know that, whatsoever God doeth, it shall be for ever: nothing can be put to it, nor any thing taken from it: and God doeth it, that men should fear before him" (Ecclesiates 3:14. KJV).

"For ye are dead, and your life is hid with Christ in God" (Colossians 3:3, KJV). Those words are God's Word—given to each of us!

Faithfulness brings a life of real peace. It is not self-created; it is God-given. As Scripture describes it, "The peace of God, which passeth all understanding, shall keep your hearts and minds through Christ Jesus" (Philippians 4:7, KJV). It is a guarding, preserving, keeping peace. It is a ruling peace: "Let the peace of God rule in your hearts, to the which also ye are called in one body; and be ye thankful" (Colossians 3:15, KJV). And that is a beautiful peace to have.

Joseph had it. I think God put that story about Joseph in the Bible for more than a history lesson. Joseph had his share of troubles. He was sold as a slave, yet God used his slavery to give him a useful life. He was thrown into jail for being morally upright, but God brought him out and gave him authority. Joseph could have lamented that he was taken from his homeland and family. But God used it for good.

Daniel had it. He lived during the reign of three kings. With each of them there was the opportunity to compromise or surrender his faith. In the lions' den, he could have wondered if it pays to be faithful to the living God. Yet there was a calm about Daniel. He knew how to live because he knew God. When Darius warned against praying to God, Daniel prayed anyway. He did what he had always done in his many years of faithful walking with God. Daniel didn't have to struggle; he just prayed. It was Darius who had to struggle with the results, who had to try to figure out some way to save Daniel from the den of lions. It was Darius who wrestled and fretted and sweated it out and found no escape from his own decree. It was Daniel, not Darius, who was the resting one.

Jesus said, "If anyone would come after me, he must deny himself and take up his cross and follow me" (Mark 8:34, NIV). The stress is on the "if." We have to weigh carefully what that "if" means. Then in response to that "if," we make a choice. But once the weighing of the consequences of that "if" has ended and the choice is made, we do not also weigh the value or the desirability of taking up the cross and following after him. Having decided to follow, we follow. Nothing less will do.

There is often misunderstanding about this matter of obeying God to the death. People without Christ see that as some kind of a religious martyr's wish, an attempt to try to please God by self-sacrifice, some kind of merit-earning. It isn't that at all. The unsaved doesn't understand. When he hears the word "sacrifice," he thinks that this is something that we do in our Christian walk. It is not something that we do in our Christian walk, it is something that may come to us because of our Christian walk. We neither look for it nor avoid it. Our commitment is to Jesus Christ, wherever that commitment leads.

If we try to suffer, to go without for the sake of going without, we are only drawing attention to ourselves. That isn't discipleship.

Dietrich Bonhoeffer said, "Our task is simply to keep on following, looking only to our Leader who goes on before, taking no notice of ourselves or of what we are doing."

The non-Christian—and even some weak Christians—marvel at this. But such obedience is not something extraordinary. It is something that Jesus' followers do. Those who choose not to follow Jesus are the "unusual" ones. They have decided against being what God created us all to be—his. They are the extraordinary ones. If indeed we who are followers are "a peculiar people," we are peculiar only to those who are not obedient.

God is building his new community. People are saying yes to Jesus Christ and yes to living the full and well-balanced life regardless of where that leads. But because of this there is opposition too. The number of martyrs around the world is increasing to the point where it is not something that surprises Christians any more. It is a fact of life.

As we begin faithfully to follow the Lord Jesus, we

may sometimes walk a stony path. But that doesn't stop us from asking each day, "How can I be faithful to you?"

It is time for each of us to make the decision about whom we will follow. Jesus does not call us to have the faith of some other person, to imitate the obedience of others, or to be disciples like them. He calls each of us to himself: "Follow me!"

That is not to say that in our individual decisions to obey we can ignore the brethren. For the Church is a body of believers. I am strengthened by this larger body. When someone else is hurt, I hurt. When someone else is destroyed, something in me is destroyed. But yet, in another sense, I am not destroyed, for Jesus still has me. No matter what happens to me or to others, it still comes to: "What is that to thee? follow thou me" (John 21:22, KJV).

We are told to take no thought for tomorrow. We are told to look at the lilies of the field and the birds of the air, and we have the example of the children of Israel in the wilderness being fed every day. We must not grab for ourselves, but at the same time we should enjoy what he provides. We must not worship what he gives, but we should worship God who gives it. And because he is meeting our needs today as he said he would, we do not worry about his faithfulness tomorrow.

The chief end of man, as the shorter catechism states it, is to enjoy God and serve him forever. That means that regardless of what happens to me, I can will to live a life of obedience. That means "Christ in me" is worked out in holiness because in keeping with Galatians 2:20, I am dead; he is alive in me. And he can do no other than to live in me a holy life, for that is what he is—holy.

I wrote in *Decision* magazine: "Holiness means to be God's, no matter what that may come to in our lives; whether we 'mount up with wings as eagles' (Isaiah 40:31, KJV), or lose our heads to a madman as did John the Baptist. Holiness is built on a pledge that I am his, a vow that is unbreakable, one in which there are no option clauses. Holiness is obedience without conditions. It is living a life that acknowledges what is true—that God is absolute Lord—a truth that is not to be violated or debated. . . . His working in the world and in our lives is not just for us and for our satisfaction, but for him, his purpose and his plans.

"Holiness means following, being ready to know his plan if he chooses to reveal it, even wishing to know his plan but not requiring to know anymore than a child who cannot comprehend all that is happening around him even when his father tries to explain it to him. The child trusts, and hand in hand he and his father go on together; the father knowing the direction, the child content to know that his father knows. It is an act of surrender.

"James H. McConkey has asked, 'What is this act of surrender? It is a yielding of the life to God to do and suffer all his will in all things and at all times because we have, once for all, settled that it is the best thing for us.'

"God may not, in the working out of his good plan, give to us what we call benefits or successes or pleasures or joys. He doesn't have to. He is God; and we may never see how our obedience works for good, either now or later because we are not God. He alone knows and comprehends all things. We are his in order to live as his—that is the essence of holiness.

"Hudson T. Armerding said, 'Let us ask ourselves whether we serve the Lord merely because he blesses us or because he is Lord. And if he is Lord, can we not trust him to do the very best for his glory and for our benefit? Indeed we can.'

"He is God, we never are and never will be, even when we are with him and like him." We are called to obey. We are called to serve. That is mature Christianity.

The day before Christmas we had a clean-up time at our house. Assignments were given and our teen-aged children went to work. They did exactly what they were told to do. "Dust the living room." They did. But no one said to throw away the scraps of things, so they were left there. "Clean the bath-room." They did, but only what was pointed out, nothing more. "Wash the kitchen floor." But no one mentioned specifically the dirty dishes in the sink. By afternoon the dishes were still there.

"Typical teenagers," people say. "They never do anything more than is absolutely required. Then they run for their rooms and put on the stereo headphones so that they can't hear the others working." But look at us. We make the same allowances for ourselves as Christians. We are "teenagers" too, doing exactly what God's law says, but nothing more. We may do enough to keep "peace" because we don't want God to be angry, but never more. Stick to the letter of the law, we say, and God won't find fault. Like teen-agers, we say to God, "But you didn't tell me to do that. I would have done it if you had told me to."

110

There should come a time when we outgrow the teen years as believers and disciples. Is God waiting for that time in your life? When did you last pick up "the dishcloth" for Christ, not because he commanded you but because you love him?

Jesus Christ is Lord. We have made our pledge to him and there are no qualifications or escape clauses to that pledge. For the one who is a Christian there can be no more filtering his commands through our preferences or trying to see how little we can do as his children. Instead there is the living-out of a sincere yes in faithfulness. This is a holy privilege.

What does this mean for each of us? James McConkey said, "Consecration, then, does not confer ownership; it presumes it. It is not in order to be His, but because we are His, that we yield up our lives. It is purchase that gives title; delivery simply gives possession."

You are a person made in the image of God. You were designed for God. You were purchased by him. To say, "I will be his regardless," is not to quit life or to say I will suffer despite my own feelings. It is to say I am his regardless of what my feelings are, whether good or bad. Philip Doddridge said, "If it is thus that my faith must be exercised, by walking in darkness for days, and months, and years to come, how long soever they may seem, how long soever they may be, I will submit."

To say I will submit regardless is not weakness; it is not fatalism. It is a grasp at last of the reality of whose people we are. It is saying, "I understand me in the context of You." It is agreeing with God in everything: to be willing not to demand that God limit himself to being no more than I am but rather to move into the fullness of the God who knows all about his creation, his world, his universe, his time, his history, his children—to say, "Regardless, I will be his."

John Calvin said, "Christian freedom is, in all its parts, a spiritual thing. . . . We have never been forbidden to laugh, or to be filled, or to join new possessions to old. . . . But where there is plenty, to wallow in delights, to gorge oneself, to intoxicate mind and heart with present pleasures and be always panting after new ones—such are very far removed from the lawful use of God's gifts.

"Away, then, with uncontrolled desire, away with immoderate prodigiality, away with vanity and arrogance—in order that men may with a clear conscience cleanly use God's gifts. . . . It is the part of a godly man to realize that free power in outward matters has been given him in order that he may be the more ready for all the duties of love."

G. Steinberger said, "We have enough people to do great things; but who is willing to do the little things? Begin with the little things, and you will not only find enough work but also harvest a blessing."

There is a stimulus to this kind of living and it comes from a willingness to be dead to ourselves and alive in Christ so that our rejoicing is not determined by that in which difficulty is absent but that in which true life is present. As realists, we understand that only as we face who we are and what we are can we begin to enjoy and live and be satisfied in the fullness and power of God. Then, in obedience, we can walk in his perfect will for us, regardless. We can do it because in Christ we are indeed "new creations." We are able to say with Philip Doddridge, "I would not merely consecrate unto thee some of my powers, or some of my possessions; or give thee a certain proportion of my services, or all I am capable of for a limited time; but I would be wholly thine, and thine forever. . . . I leave, O Lord, to thy management and direction, all I possess, and all I wish; and set every enjoyment and every interest before thee, to be disposed of as thou pleasest."

Will we say that? Will we mean it? Regardless?

What will be the result? At long last God will be free to do what he has always wanted to do in each of our lives. He will have that chance to supply our every need "according to his riches in glory by Christ Jesus" (Philippians 4:19, KJV).

And God will!

# EIGHT
# And God Will

† *God will meet all your needs according to his glorious riches in Christ Jesus* [Philippians 4:19, NIV].

If there is a single desperate need that people have right now, it is not the need for more education, it is not the need for more money, it is not the need for greater security—it is the need to lay claim to this: "God will!"

When we look at who God is, when we look at what he gives, when we look at what he says, then we can believe, "God will meet all your needs." For our God delivers on his promises:

"I will never leave thee, nor forsake thee" (Hebrews 13:5, KJV)—that's a promise!

"I am with you alway, even unto the end of the world" (Matthew 28:20, KJV)—that's a promise too!

"Trust in the Lord with all thine heart; and lean not unto thine own understanding. In all thy ways acknowledge him, and he shall direct thy paths" (Proverbs 3:5, 6, KJV)—he will; he says so!

"Commit thy way unto the Lord; trust also in him; and he shall bring it to pass" (Psalm 37:5, KJV)—God will!

"If ye shall ask any thing in my name, I will do it"

(John 14:14, KJV)—"I will!" he said.

"Him that cometh to me I will in no wise cast out" (John 6:37, KJV)—we have his word on it.

"And ye shall know the truth, and the truth shall make you free" (John 8:32, KJV)—you shall!

"His divine power hath given unto us all things that pertain unto life and godliness, through the knowledge of him that hath called us to glory and virtue" (2 Peter 1:3, KJV)—he said "all things," and he means it.

"The eternal God is thy refuge, and underneath are the everlasting arms" (Deuteronomy 33:27, KJV)—and that's his promise too.

But don't stop with these few promises; get your own Bible and keep discovering more of his promises thoughtfully and prayerfully! You will find that God is much involved with you. Can you believe that? God has given his Word, his promise, his commitment, and as Emile Cailliet says in his book *Journey Into Light,* "Indeed God stands behind the Book."

"His Book" is the revelation of himself; he acts on it. "His Book" doesn't lie; God always keeps his word. Only God can rightly speak about himself and properly interpret the holy things that are his. For his ways defy our human speculation. In this world, in spite of our human disorientation, there is a standard that does not change: the Holy Scripture. Scripture is God's statement. He proclaims and he practices what he proclaims.

When we allow ourselves to accept his word, rejoice in his word, and determine to obey his word, then everything that we do will take on new dimensions of meaning.

That means we can look at our failures and understand them; we can learn from each one. That means we can make decisions in the assurance that God is the over-all ruler of our lives, even if we make what we call a "bad" decision. That means we no longer have to live with questions about what could have been, but are able to experience life with the One who is the God of life and the overseer of the great friendship that he has established with us, a friendship far greater than we can comprehend. We can worship him and love him always because God will always be God and he will always care—he promised that! In Jesus Christ, we are "best friends" with God.

And as God's "friend," I can say with excitement, "You are my God," even though I cannot fully comprehend that. I can acknowledge, "You have waiting for me far more than I could ever give to myself." For that I can truly thank him.

It is not mere existence that I celebrate, it is life. And I can celebrate that life whether mine is a life of great accomplishment or a life with no measurable results. It is within the excitement of the life he gives to me, his gift to me, that I worship him and yield myself to him.

Do you deserve this? Are you asking, "How can God be that way?" You could consume hours, even years, on that question, wasting potentially creative energy in pondering yourself and God, his nature and the meaning of all his love for you. But you don't need to understand it. God's love, will, and direction is not conditional on whether or not you understand it or on what you think about it; it is conditional on him, the ever steady omnipotent One, and on your response in faith to him.

"Well, then," you may be asking, "is this the ultimate, the highest goal? Am I to seek God's will so that I can attain more of what I want?" No! Some try to do that. They think, "Since God wants me to be fulfilled and happy, I'll claim God." They go through believing-type motions and then wonder, "Why am I not fulfilled? Is this all there is to the so-called expanded life?" They are not surrendering to God; they are merely trying to use God, and God will not be used.

To have God is to enjoy him; that's completion, that's fulfillment, that's happiness. But he is not a magic "happiness giver." In him we have a happy life because happiness is a by-product of the God-centered life. Ours is a happy life, a larger share of life, because we have in us the One who is life and complete happiness.

Do you want to have that larger share of living? Then know this: God wants you to have it too!

Come away from the notion that this is some kind of self-improvement plan. True discipleship can't be a self-improvement program. Unfortunately, even some Christians misunderstand that. Their "me-and-God" views have been kept alive by the flood of books on the Christian market listing "how to," "you can be," "steps to," and although many of these books have good biblical resource material, and while the intentions of the authors are sincere, there are some negative aspects too. One is the implication that if we do various things that are taught in these books we will somehow live as close to Jesus as the examples given in the books, or be as successful, or as attractive, or will have a no-conflict marriage, or will find ourselves in circumstances like those of the authors. The second implication is that *we* are the faith-generators. We find ourselves saying, "I must have faith," and focus our attention on the program or the steps to faith, and not on Jesus himself. We become people who follow the teachings about Christ when we should be following the teachings of Christ.

Jesus knows where I am. He knows my circumstances. And although good teaching and good examples can be found among other members within the body, my eyes are not to be on the other members only but on the One who knows me, who put me together, who wants me to be conformed to his likeness. I learn through others, but what I learn is about the Lord Jesus Christ himself and how better to live for him. I learn theologically, I learn systematically, I learn doctrinally, and it all comes together in him.

There are frustrated Christians who have been pushed or coaxed into a self-remodeling program that denies the fact that we are not our own. It is by grace that we are saved, it is not of ourselves, and it is by the grace of God and his direction that we become like him. And all of the teaching, all of the books, all of the lectures—though they can give good information—only make sense when they are incorporated into the leading of God for our lives. We must first be committed to our Lord, and be willing to be what he wants us to be. Then the other teachings make sense.

When the Teton Dam in Idaho burst on June 5, 1976, a wall of water swept down the valley tearing out homes and barns, crumpling farm machinery, and tossing heavy equipment everywhere. A few days later, when the water had receded, twisted trees and dead animals were strewn everywhere, and mud and gravel lay several feet thick over everything.

Ten months after that flood I visited a Christian

family who lived there. In the flood they lost everything. But when I arrived, they had already rebuilt their house, bought new farm equipment, erected new buildings, and had scraped the gravel deposits off their land. They were ready to plant. Yet all around them were neighbors who had done nothing. Many of these neighbors were religious people who had built up those farms by hard work. But after the dam broke, they were left without hope. What they had built was theirs; now it was gone. Most had not even scraped the thick gravel deposits from their land. They were still dazed. They couldn't function. They stood helpless. What was "theirs" was gone, and they couldn't handle it.

What was the difference? Though the dam break was said to be caused by human error in construction, the Christian family continued to hang on to Romans 8:28, believing that God knew what was happening. Their house and farm belonged to God before the flood, and it was his afterward. They started to rebuild even before the water receded. They had a sense of direction, clinging to the belief that God would use this for good. Now in their home there is a growing house church; they are ministering to other people. When the flood came, those whose religion was based on "God helping me" were devastated. The Christians believed "God owns me" and were able to function. Good or bad times were not critical to their foundation of faith.

Such severe crises don't come to everybody, but if they do come, the self-improved, self-developed "religious" people often have nothing left. A person who has only his own version of the empowering God has no power at all.

During good times, the true disciple and the simply religious person are not too distinguishable. The differences are inside. But when crises come (and sooner or later they usually do) the one embarked on the "foolish adventure" of being totally yielded to Christ has the strength to endure.

Consider Psalm 5:8. David prayed, "Make thy way straight before my face" (KJV). If you are like some people, you probably learned that verse the other way around: "Make my way straight before thy face." That's because those who are religious on their own terms have learned to pray, "Lord, I want what I am doing to be right with you; I want to please you with what I am and where I am going; I seek your blessing on my life." In other words, "Make *my* way straight before *thy* face"—be pleased with where *I* am going. But David prayed the other way. He prayed that God's way would be straight before him so that he could follow it. The focus of the true believer is on God's way—wherever God's way leads, that is the way the committed believer will go.

Discipleship is a coming under the guidance and the control of the Master Engineer, the Craftsman of the Universe, the Divine Potter. At times it means being thrown hard on the Potter's wheel. Sometimes it means being pressed or even pounded under the hand of God. Sometimes it means being firmly held while the wheel turns. That reshaping and remaking goes on and on, according to the Potter's plan. The clay doesn't say, "Please bless the object I'm about to become as I shape my life." The clay is clay; it becomes something according to the Potter's idea of what it should be. The results that come are what the Potter wants.

121

It's the same as the cutting and pruning that Jesus talked about in referring to his Father as the Vine-dresser. The vine doesn't flourish by its own strength, nor is it necessarily a better vine for spreading out everywhere. It is the cutting, the shaping, and the pruning that produces fruit. It's the Vinedresser's doing, not the plant's. The plant doesn't say, "Let my pruning be pleasing to you," or, "Bless the pruning I do on myself." The plant submits.

Christian maturing means a day-by-day following and obedience, a being available, ready. When the Apostle Paul wrote to the Christians at Rome he told them, "I wanted to come to you but was hindered. I had to go in another direction, but I'm going to come to you now on the way to Spain" (see Romans 15:22–24). But he never got to Spain! When he finally saw the Christians at Rome, he was in chains. He came as a prisoner, which was not at all what he had planned. Yet there was no panic in Paul's writing or in his life. In the relaxed awareness that "God owns me," all things did work together for good. He was not a man serving God on his terms or by his own plan; he served God on God's terms, by God's plan. He said elsewhere, "I know both how to be abased, and I know how to abound" (Philippians 4:12, KJV). He knew he was being led, and he used his prison time to minister, since that's where he was, just as he would have ministered if he were free. He didn't give up. He made his plans for Spain; those plans didn't work out. Yet he wasn't disappointed. His attention was focused on God.

For a lot of people, if what happened to Paul happened to them they would be emotionally or spiritually crippled. If life doesn't go the way they plan, they collapse. "But I prayed about it," they say. Paul prayed about Spain, too. "I felt led," they say. Paul did too, or he wouldn't have started out for Spain. But always, Paul was a man of God. He was a follower.

God is building a people for himself, a people willing to obey and follow. Maybe the hardest thing for you to realize right now is that at this moment he is building *you*. We like to say, "Ah, yes, look at what God did to make a John Wesley or a William Booth." We like to hear about their conversion to Christ and how God led them. Stories of Wesley and Booth are beautiful and true, and we need the encouragement and the inspiration that come from their stories, but there is a point that is often missed. We overlook God's current miracle. The miracle is not only that God did something radical in the lives of the famous. The miracle is that he is working a great change in each of us too.

Insecure Christians are great at trotting out Christians who are successful and famous, almost as if it is some kind of proof that God is powerful. We point to the Christian entertainer as if he is more "proof" of God's power than the Christian factory worker. Or we take a newly converted sensation and tout him as evidence of the "wonderful grace of Jesus." Many of our church conference planners would never have allowed Saul of Tarsus to go off for those silent but important years while God shaped him into Paul the missionary. They would have had him in their pulpits, or pushed him to write a book, long before he was ready. He would have been urged to sign autographs for people who need to say to their friends, "I know him."

The titillating, the sensational, the vicarious enjoyment of prestige really points to the weakness in our own relationship to God. It shows that we do not know who we are. The confessed sin of a thief or prostitute doesn't need to be savored again and again for those who really know Christ—they don't need celebrity examples to be certain that God is God. The power of God is amply proven in what he is doing right now in our lives.

Our own discipleship must be a daily matter for prayer. We do not point to ourselves in pride or feel that we have arrived, because we know that we can fall any minute; many have. A. H. McNeile warned himself and in doing so warns us: "Everyone in my home, my office, my place of business, my school, knows that I care about religion. And I do care; I care intensely; I really don't think I could betray my Lord. And yet—'the hand of him that betrayeth Me is with Me on the Table'; 'Mine own familiar friend, whom I trusted.'"

And C. S. Lewis said, "When we Christians behave badly, or fail to behave well, we are making Christianity unbelievable to the outside world. The wartime posters told us that Careless Talk Costs Lives. It is equally true that Careless Lives Cost Talk. Our careless lives set the outer world talking, and we give them grounds for·talking in a way that throws doubt on the truth of Christianity itself."

Like Peter, I slip back and I surge forward. I might be a failure in some areas, a success in others, but always I must trust that God has me, and I must not stray from him. It is so easy to slip.

The temptation to slip can even creep up on those who are mature in the faith and have a strong witness.

When people come to appreciate how God is using a particular man or a woman, they pray for him or her. That is the right thing to do. If we see that God is working through a person, we bring our neighbors and friends under his ministry so more people are blessed and fed. Again, we should do that. But Satan gets in there too and will try to tell the prayed-for Christian leader that the gifts and power evidenced in his life are his own. If the Christian leader ever starts to take credit for what God is doing through him, or if he forgets that what God is doing is in answer to the prayers of the faithful, he can fall, bringing great shame to the Christian Church and dishonor to the name he bears. That person may still go on being an instrument in the hand of God, because God is still answering the prayers of others, choosing to use him in spite of himself. But someday, however long it takes, he will answer for his straying and for trying to steal God's glory. God warned, "I will not give my glory unto another" (Isaiah 48:11, KJV). God will be God; he may use an "unjust prophet" for awhile, but someday that will end. We must never forget that.

The adventure of following Jesus Christ on his terms and for his glory means that it really isn't important whether we have ten talents or one so long as God can use for himself the talents he gives. They are his gift, to be used for his sake. It is blasphemy to take any credit for what he is doing in us or with us.

Moses had an intimate relationship with God, but he didn't try to take credit for his usefulness nor brag about his power—he knew that it wasn't his own.

He could argue with God (Exodus 5:22, 23), and God with him; they were that close. But in Moses God knew that he had a man who wasn't self-seeking.

125

That's the kind of person God looks for today too.

When it comes time to lead people out of the wilderness, God doesn't call an egotistical Pharisee to do it. He calls one who recognizes the cloud and pillar of fire for what they are—God's leading—one who is willing to put one foot in front of the other and follow because God said to do so. God has never changed his standards.

We have our human standards for who is "great," but they don't impress God. We have our measure for those who are "more useful" than others, but God doesn't measure that way. Paul, a man God used, made it clear that some may plant and some may water, but it is always God who gives the increase. A farmer doesn't spend all of his time harvesting. There is a time for harvest, but only because there was first the planting, and because God gave the increase.

I remember as a new Christian that I tried to witness to another student at Wayne State University. I wasn't happy about what I said to him. I felt that I hadn't said things correctly. It wasn't a polished presentation of the gospel, and I was only able to tell him a little bit about the Good News. I did not lead him to faith in Christ.

But God was in it, and perhaps in order to teach me he showed me something special about that witness. A few days after that conversation, another student said to me, "Do you know Tom came to Christ yesterday?" There were five or six of us sitting together when he said that, and together we rejoiced over the news. In particular, we expressed our gratitude for the man who introduced Tom to Christ. But then somebody said, "I spoke to Tom a couple of weeks ago, and this is what I said." Then somebody else added that he too had spoken to Tom about Christ.

As we talked and compared notes, we began to see what had happened. Each of us, without knowing about the others, had witnessed to Tom. None of us had felt that we had been successful or even complete in our witness. Yet as we checked what each had said and the time when we said it, we found that God had led Tom to each of us, and each one in sequence had picked up where the other had left off. Without knowing it, each of us had given Tom one more piece of the gospel message, the next step, until finally the last man led him into the kingdom.

Who was the soul-winner? None of us! It was the Holy Spirit's doing. Sometimes I may be allowed to do the harvesting, sometimes I may do the planting; most of the time my job is to help dig out the weeds or carry the water. We do what has to be done, directed by the One who owns the field. But we will do our job successfully only to the degree that we keep our eyes on the Master and do as we're told.

Get close to God. Listen to him. Let his Word become a part of you, and watch what he does with your life. Then no matter what happens, wherever you go, whatever you do, the deep-down peace that comes with obedience will be yours. During your lifetime you will have the joy of seeing Jesus use you. And some day you will have something extra, something special; you will hear those words which none of us can say to ourselves: "Well done, thou good and faithful servant . . . enter thou into the joy of thy lord" (Matthew 25:21, KJV).

We have the guidance of our Namesake—we are Christ-ones—because we live in God's will. In God's will I no longer need to be dominated by fear. In

God's will I can practice my true humanity without trying to be superspiritual. In God's will I am free to be me, for I am alive. And in God's will there is pleasure even in doing ordinary things because God is in the ordinary just as much as he is in the spectacular. As Saint Francis learned, the mundane can be enjoyed. We can happily wash the pots and pans in Jesus' name.

To be in God's will doesn't mean that we have all things going smoothly. In fact, it is neither biblical nor true that those who have little trouble are blessed and those who have much trouble are not. Jesus made that clear; he talked about the rich man and Lazarus and the crumbs from the table. How foolish to think that someone who struggles with cancer or poverty or unexciting work is less of a saint. God is the Sanctifier. He is the King, and the King gives the orders. We are to follow those orders. We are in his army whether we carry the flag or clean the garbage cans. Be sure that you are in his will where he wants you. Be sure daily that you have sought that place of faithfulness. Jesus said, "Ye are my friends, if ye do whatsoever I command you" (John 15:14, KJV). Be sure that you are his friend.

By God's will I can function according to his greatness, not according to my thoughts about a given situation. In him I may cry in my own pain, but will also cry when I see the suffering of others. In God's will I will not be always judging my gift or his use of it, whether I have been given something large or small, whether that gift is for myself or to offer to a person who is hurting: a cup of cold water, a word of encouragement, or a piece of bread. By God's will I am here to give. In the Church, which is a hospital, I may not be the surgeon but I may be an orderly. And as an orderly for Jesus, I have something to do for this sick world.

Richard Baxter in 1650 said that too. "The church on earth is a mere hospital. Which way ever we go, we hear complaining, and into what corner soever we cast our eyes, we behold objects of pity and grief. . . . Who weeps not when all these bleed? As now our friends' distresses are our distresses, so then our friends' deliverance will be part of our own deliverance. . . . How much more comfortable to see them perfected, than now to see them wounded, weak, sick and afflicted? . . . . Our day of rest will free both them and us from all this."

But until that day of rest comes, we will—we must—minister in Jesus' name out of the wealth of all that he has given to us. It may be tough, but God is tough too.

John Haggai once stated, "If our path had been smooth, we might have depended upon our own surefootedness. Perhaps God roughened the path so we would take hold of His hand. If the weather had been mild, we might have loitered along the beach."

To be his is to understand that we can work for Christ and rest in Christ, for both activities are ours in him. A Marine wading ashore during an invasion does not do it so that he will have a place to lie down and get a suntan; he does it to conquer. But later, at another time or in another situation, he can just as faithfully take that rest and get a suntan. In Christ there is a time for the Christian to do both.

Living in God's will means that we can know that he is in charge when we are hard at work, and have the peace of knowing that he is also in charge when we are playing golf or are in bed with the flu. In hard work or soft rest we can enjoy him. We can live every day by God's will and God's leading.

I can enjoy him when I am working to help people or when I ignore the clamoring multitude, as Jesus sometimes did, to go aside and pray. For in both, Jesus was obedient. There is no guilt associated with such obedience. We can say with Philip Doddridge, "Thou reignest and I rejoice in it, as it is indeed a matter of universal joy. I believe thy universal providence and care; and I firmly believe thy wise, holy and kind interposition in every thing which relates to me, and to the circumstances of my abode in this thy world."

And in his *Testament of Devotion,* Thomas Kelly said, "Walk and talk and work and laugh with your friends. But behind the scenes, keep up the life of simple prayer and inward worship. Keep it up throughout the day. Let inward prayer be your last act before you fall asleep and the first act when you awake. And in time you will find as did Brother Lawrence, that 'those who have the gale of the Holy Spirit go forward even in sleep.' "

So much depends on our willingness to trust and follow. Don't ever measure the meaning of a day by the content of that day. No matter what, God is God. The Bible states, "He that keepeth Israel shall neither slumber nor sleep" (Psalm 121:4, KJV). And if you want to see how obedience and design come together, read the scope of history in Acts 7, then ask yourself, "Do I want my time in history to be the same?"

Scripture assures that God is "thinking about me constantly. . . . And when I waken in the morning, you are still thinking of me" (Psalm 139:17, 18, TLB). E. M. Bounds in *Power Through Prayer* said, "God can work wonders if He can get a suitable man. Men can work wonders if they can get God to lead them." Thus being in God's will is the greatest work that I can do even if sometimes it is doing nothing. I can honor him as much in trusting rest as in great works. For trust is what causes us to treat him as he is—God. And our God is great!

Cameron Thompson said, "We need to ask according to His greatness and not according to the feebleness of our desires. One who asked an incredible boon of Napoleon had it immediately granted because, said Napoleon, 'He honored me by the magnitude of his request.'"

Trust him, ask of him, seek from him, look to him, enjoy him, serve him with obedience knowing that he will provide. Rest in him knowing that he will provide, claim his promises knowing that he will provide. He is our God; we are his people. God is for us. He is on our side. As Presbyterian author and editor George Laird Hunt assures us, "The great divorce cannot happen."

How much larger this kind of living is than the shallow belief that if I do "my" part, God will do his part, as if we live by some kind of divine trade-off. His will is bigger than just giving to me. His will for me—and for all of us—is for his honor and for his kingdom.

Let us long to be in him and in his will and to be his people. That for now and always is the very best there is. F. P. Harton said, "The soul loves to do the will of God because it is His. God's commands are not an unwelcome imposition, but the way in which the soul may please Him, and so the soul gladly and lovingly submits itself to them.''

In his will we are ready for anything that God cares to do with us. He knows us. Most of all, he gives of himself to us because he knows that as obedient disciples we are able to be trusted.

# NINE
# Able to Be Trusted

*† Therefore . . . be ye stedfast, unmoveable, always abounding in the work of the Lord, forasmuch as ye know that your labour is not in vain in the Lord* [1 Corinthians 15:58, KJV].

In 1917, A. H. McNeile, Fellow of Sidney Sussex College, Cambridge, wrote: "It has been said that 'humility is the truth about ourselves.*' And the truth about ourselves is just what we find it so hard to see. Ask God with all your might to enable you to say, 'One thing I know, that whereas I was blind, now I see.' Now I see why I could not overcome that temptation; I thought I was safe enough without constant watching; I thought I could get along all right without daily self-examination; I thought I could get forgiveness although I had not really and sincerely confessed my sins; I thought I could grow in grace without growing in prayerfulness."

If I am God's person, if I live my life in him and find my satisfaction in him, can God trust me? Can I be trusted as a person who is wholly his, trusted as an ambassador, trusted as a witness to Jesus Christ, trusted as a friend of God?

I am not removed from the corruption of this

world. I am not suspended in a cocoon-type state of artificial holiness. I am not "holier than thou," but I can live a holy life within the pleasure of his company in this world with all of its pain and sordidness and misery. And you can too.

All of us, in our honest times, have to say truthfully, "I am not what I ought to be." And we might be tempted to be forever worried about that. But we can't, not if we understand forgiveness—the meaning of forgotten sin. Instead, each of us has to go on in confidence in the promise, "If we confess our sins, he is faithful and just to forgive us our sins, and to cleanse us from all unrighteousness" (1 John 1:9, KJV), and live out what we are—forgiven ones, always keeping short accounts with God, always remembering what we might have been without both the liberation and the restraints of the love and law of God.

Do people know that God owns me? Do they know that in my attempts to practice the presence of God I am not trying to show off to them or to impress them? Do they know that what I want for myself and for them is the greatest good, God's best?

We are not safe from failure so long as our feet are in this clay called "the world." We will always be tempted; sometimes we will fall down. Yet can we be trusted because God knows that we want to obey him and because people sense that Christ can have his way in our lives?

Not long ago someone said to me, "You are one of the most moral men I know." At first that statement stunned me. Then the seriousness of it almost destroyed me. What an "awful" thing for someone to say. I went home and told Andrea what this person said. Without looking up from the stove where she was stirring something she said, "Well, you are a moral man," and went on with her cooking. That frightened me still more. It is not that I prefer to be immoral; I don't. But I fear being thought of as moral because of the dangers it can bring. I have great weaknesses, temptations; it would take only a second to slip. In my praying I keep facing that. Am I moral in my views about the people around me? Am I moral in my treatment of persons of another culture or race? Am I moral in my attitude toward material things and my consumption of them; the way I handle money or food or resources? Am I moral in my political stand? Am I moral toward my children and their values? Am I moral toward my family, including my larger Christian family? Am I moral in my behavior toward my wife and the life God has given her to live? Am I moral in my thinking and in my dreaming and in my planning? Am I moral in my worship? Can I be trusted, morally, with the name "Christian"?

Not long after I was called a "moral" man, I was requested by my staff to write an article on holiness. I knew that I could write it journalistically. I knew, too, that I could write it biblically and practically. But could I handle the subject personally? Did I have the right to put my thoughts on paper, to make a declaration, to take a stand before others?

I asked my staff, "What if I slip? What if I write about holiness and tomorrow I fall prey to my own temptations? What if I am not in fact living what I write about?" The people heard me out. Then one of them said pointedly, "Well, then you're defeated already."

And that is correct. For no one writes, or lives, or acts out of his wholeness. He writes, lives, and acts out of his weakness. It is because we are incomplete that we can seek to be holy and to be trusted. We are obedient not because we have arrived at perfection, for none of us has, but because we haven't, and we cry to God for help. F. P. Harton explained it: "Christian morality is, fundamentally, obedience to the revealed will of an holy God."

C. S. Lewis said, "Does it not make a great difference whether I am, so to speak, the landlord of my own mind and body or only a tenant, responsible to the real landlord? If somebody else made me for his own purposes, then I shall have a lot of duties which I should not have if I simply belonged to myself." Because I have chosen to be called by the name Christian, I have a terrible responsibility to serve him and to be his person.

The moment I say I am a Christian, I am declaring that I am a disciple, a follower: "I am crucified with Christ" (Galatians 2:20, KJV). I am saying that I am not my own, that I am bought with a price. Christ is in me.

To be a Christian is a frightening responsibility; yet how can one ever be trusted if he is always burdened by the problems he might encounter? Harry A. Ironsides clarified this for me: "No one will ever know down here the full results of a life lived wholly for God and a will fully yielded to Him. The effects on all with whom such a surrendered believer associates are incalculable in their peace-giving power. On the other hand, no one can tell until the secret things are revealed in the day of the revelation of Jesus Christ, how much harm a restless, quarrelsome, critical. fault-finding person can do in the way of disturbing the peace of any group with which such a dissatisfied, selfish soul mingles. We are all either helpers in the things which make for peace or we are assisting in spreading unrest and disturbance, which dishonors the Lord, grieves the Holy Spirit and hinders the work of winning the lost to Jesus Christ."

Can I be trusted? Do people know that in the deepest part of my heart I want to follow Christ? Not that there will be a holy aura emanating from me, but is my desire something that is noted just as much as one notes that I am a certain weight or height or that I walk a particular way? Is this life in Christ as much a part of me as my likes, my tastes, my way of acting? Is it just as clear as anything else about me that I want to be his?

This is critically important because Christians know inside whether or not they sincerely want to follow Jesus or if they only want to talk about following Jesus. And others know too; they can tell. Sometimes those who talk most noisily about following Jesus do not communicate that they are following him. Can you be trusted to be a follower of Jesus— even when no one is looking?

Do people know that in your time alone with God you struggle too, as they do, that sometimes you argue with God about the worth of your life? Do they know that you are up and down, as they are, not having "made it" but always wanting to be better? You may not win all your battles, but do you long to win them in Christ and for Christ? Do people know that even your failures are your teachers to help you toward a closer walk with God?

Can you be trusted to seek out other people for the Savior? Do people who want to find God know that they can talk to you about him? Do your neighbors know that? They may tease you about it, but do they know that you genuinely love God and long to have them know God too? Are you honest with them about that?

Can you be trusted to tell the truth about God, or do you hedge and sidestep? When was the last time you tried to speak to someone about the Lord Jesus? In one of the early draft papers presented at the Consultation on World Evangelization at Pattaya, Thailand, June 1980, was the statement: "The secular man's deepest need is to discover that he is meant to be a redeemed child of God. He is not a complete, fulfilled human being. Although a season of 'temporary euphoria' in the lives of many other secular people around him will convince him that they are 'moving up the ladder,' have 'got their act together,' and 'have got it made'—time and events inevitably cause them to come down off their 'secular high' and face their finitude. The secularized man's felt needs —loneliness, emptiness, fear, guilt, meaninglessness, and a search for peace, love and joy—will only be satisfied when he encounters Jesus Christ and commits himself personally to Him. This encounter transforms a life of frustration, superficiality, despair and ultimate judgment. At this point, his unperceived need for self-esteem will be realized. He can live for God's glory, to know, love and obey Him and to serve his fellowman."

We must not pretend that people do not want or need Jesus. They do! One of the most hateful things that a Christian can do is to lie to another about that. Richard Baxter, writing in 1650, said: "Do not daub with men, and hide from them their misery or danger, or any part of it; do not make their sins less than they are, nor speak of them in an extenuating language; do not encourage them in a false hope or faith, no more than you would discourage the sound hopes of the righteous. If you see his case is dangerous, tell him plainly of it. . . . It is not hovering at a distance in a general discourse that will serve the turn."

Scripture says, "Wherefore he is able also to save them to the uttermost that come unto God by him, seeing he ever liveth to make intercession for them" (Hebrews 7:25, KJV). Yet there are pastors and whole congregations who keep their worship and their talk on the horizontal. They say, "Worship is what happens between us because we meet together." People, empty from the pain of life and coming in hope into a church sanctuary, are kept from seeing the One who alone can save, fulfill, and offer them life. Even the Lord's Supper is sometimes relegated to the horizontal—"Because we take it together"—and is not worship in remembrance of him. This is more than a heresy problem, for it is more than doctrinal—it is a hatred toward our fellow men. It is purposely keeping people from the sure Word of love. We want people to love each other, but they won't be able to if we keep them from the Source of true love.

Can you be trusted to tell the truth honestly about God, not out of some sense of being superior, but because you sincerely long for people to know the God of truth and life? Certainly the true longing of your heart cannot be hidden.

Do people know even from your silence how much you love them for what they are now as well as for what they can be in Christ? Do people know that you will help them become God's best as they seek God's will? This does not mean that you will be in church work every moment, because some who are give the least help. It does not mean that you will always be available at every call, for sometimes you must step back in order to help the most. But do people know that you will help them, whether they call in the middle of the night or whether they take you from your fireside and family—do they know that you are available to them? Can you be trusted to go to them as Jesus went? Philip Doddridge urged, "Be an advocate for truth; be a counsellor of peace; be an example of candour; and do all you can to reconcile the hearts of men."

Can you be trusted never to disclose a confidence? Do people know that when they speak to you it will never be told? We have all been hurt, deeply hurt, by those who have promised to keep a confidence only to broadcast it.

Recently someone did that to me. He not only broke his promise, but when I told him how he had betrayed me, he proceeded to tell others what it was that hurt me and repeated my confidence again to his current audience in order to hurt even more. He is a Christian, one whom God uses in many areas of ministry, but I cannot trust him any more.

A faithful Christian who can be trusted will still sometimes be mistaken for a betrayer. You have surely had it happen that when you have kept private counsel, as you promised, the confidence has come to light through another party. You cannot convince the confider that you kept your word. You endure the pain of being thought a traitor. But God knows; he will still bring others to you when they need help because he knows you can be trusted.

Years ago my wife, Andrea, and I agreed that we

would trust each other enough to allow a ministry of counselling. That wasn't something that came out of our heads but out of a trust of the heart. We can trust each other because what we have between us is deeper and richer than anything each of us may have with another person. When people talk to me, they know that it will go no farther if they wish it not to. The same is true with Andrea. I remember once asking, quite innocently, what somebody said to her and she replied, "I cannot tell you." I was satisfied with that. Of course she could not tell me. It would have been wrong for her to tell me. It was enough that she told me that the person had a need. Trust means that there is no gossip about the subject even "for prayer." Thus a pastor or a fellow Christian can be told, knowing that it will not be a "spiritual application" in a sermon, or an announcement in a prayer meeting for all to relish and "pray about."

Can you be trusted to keep a confidence because you are secure in Jesus and don't need the reputation for being "in the know"? Can you weep and cry with an individual without him or her ever telling another about your "effective ministry"? Can you be trusted not to use people for your own ego needs?

If you have been used for someone's ego satisfaction, you know that one of the most painful things to discover is that somebody is using you. You may be in that kind of situation now. But try to be faithful. Help people in their work and ministry even if you know that they are using you to gain some benefit for themselves, or worse, are putting you out on a limb so that if it is cut off they are safe and you take the fall. Not everyone who is in Christ understands faithfulness. Some think trust is weakness and that weakness is something to be exploited for their own gain. Know that it will happen and remain faithful.

The risk that somebody will use you cannot interfere with your ministry in Christ. You can't be paranoid about people who are "out to use you." The trusting Christian knows there are some who will hurt or destroy, just as one knows that there may be dangers in walking down a street late at night. Don't let that stop you from offering your heart and help to others. Be trusted to love regardless of what people do, because in this world people are hungry to be loved. They may not know how to handle it. They may hurt you, but they need your love.

There is such fear among some Christians who have been so used and hurt that they prefer to keep relationships sterile, even cold. Even in their praying they do not really grapple with the true issues but prefer the "platform" approach to prayer where they stay impersonal, where they do not get involved.

Perhaps they are frightened that if they reach out to touch or love they will be seen as getting too close, too intimate. I have sensed it. I remember once when a young man I was trying to help made a serious commitment of his life to Jesus Christ, I hugged him. It was a major step in his life that God is now honoring, but I knew how he had struggled and wrestled for so many months before he took that step. As we embraced, I saw someone look at me with shock in his eyes and I knew immediately what he was thinking: here was a man hugging another man. He did not understand.

One Sunday I was preaching in a federal penitentiary where 95 percent of the inmates were black. I tried to explain the love and saving work of Jesus

Christ, and invited the men to respond to Christ as their Savior and Lord. I gave an altar call and then waited. No one responded. Minutes passed, and I wondered if I had failed to communicate. Then, to close the meeting, I prayed for the men. When I finished praying and opened my eyes, I saw that one man, a black man, had come to the front. I went to him, took him by the hand, and asked him about his decision. He told me that it was to present his life to Christ. I spoke to him for a minute as the rest of the men sat watching. Then, as I continued to hold his hand, I put my other arm around his shoulder and prayed that God would bless his decision and his life and use him there in the prison. When I opened my eyes and looked up, I found that thirteen more men had come forward. Later, I realized why. They had come not because of the content of the sermon but because they had seen that I truly did want that brother to be saved. I was not just a white man talking at black men, but a man who wanted another man to know Christ. I had to love him with that touch; it is my way. Could I have shown my feelings without that touch? Maybe, and some people can, but I can't—and I think it mattered that day.

The same things happen, as I learned over the years with my students, in ministering to women as well as men. It is a delicate thing, but early in my ministry I found that sometimes it was the touch of a hand or a hug that communicated most.

Sometimes I would walk the campus at night with students, men or women, or even visit them in a private place in the dormitory. It was a caring time. I would come home and tell Andrea that I was with this person or that one, and tell her what happened, without revealing a confidence. I had the security of knowing that Andrea trusted me, and because of that trust I could give myself in love to people in need. That is indeed a beautiful thing. And I've told her so.

One weekend a young woman came to us for counselling and the two of us spent several hours alone in my study. Andrea had asked ahead of time if the woman wanted to speak to both of us or just to me, and she replied that if Andrea didn't mind she would like to talk to me alone. We talked for a long time together, and she cried and we prayed. She felt so terribly separated from God, so unloved, and I was able to put my arm around her and tell her that I loved her but most of all that God loved her in spite of all that had transpired in her life. Today her feet are on the Solid Rock again and events since have borne out that she has gone on with Christ. Later I said to Andrea, "I could never have done that anywhere else. I could not put my arm around a woman who is crying lest someone read into it. I could not say, 'I love you,' except in our home where you are. But you understand, you trust, and you know that there is only one who has all of my heart and love, and that is you."

Of course we should always be aware of our weaknesses. We should be aware of lust rather than genuine love. We are to bring wholeness to people; therefore, we must never in any way hurt or use a person. Always we are to add one more part to their healing as God gives the opportunity.

Can you be trusted to work for healing? Can you help? Can you work to bring about wholeness in people, families, hurting marriages? Can you be trusted to build up the home? If God puts someone in your care, can he trust you to give what he wants that person to have from you? Are you a channel for his blessing?

Can you be trusted to fight against the things that destroy people, to work to stop the murder of people in war, the murder of the innocent unborn, or the murder of the sick and helpless?

Can you bring something richer, fuller, better into the life of each person you meet? Can you be trusted to do that? Or do you take what is lawful, what is good, what is holy, and twist it or sully it? Do you practice faith or use religion, serve God or serve the benefits that come from God? Are you capable or incapable of virtue? William Law said, "If it be asked why religion does not get possession of their hearts, the reason is this; it is not because they live in gross sins or debaucheries, for their regard to religion preserves them from such disorders; but it is because their hearts are constantly employed, perverted, and kept in a wrong state by the indiscreet use of such things as are lawful to be used. . . . Therefore it never comes into their heads to imagine any great danger from that quarter. They never reflect that there is a vain and imprudent use of their estates, which, though it does not destroy like gross sins, yet so disorders the heart, and supports it in sensuality and dulness, such pride and vanity, as makes it incapable of receiving the life and spirit of piety.

"For our souls may receive an infinite hurt and be rendered incapable of all virtue, merely by the use of innocent and lawful things."

Can you be trusted to be honest, to work hard, to give your best no matter what? When our daughter held one of her first jobs, she asked me, "How am I to work with people who tell me that I'm doing too much? When I'm through in one area, I go work in another because that's what I'm paid to do. But they say, 'You make us look bad.' " She has learned early that she will be appreciated more by some people if she cheats her employer.

Can you handle that type of response when it happens to you and still be trusted to be faithful? Will you give your employer an honest hour's work for that hour's wage? Are you responsible enough not to cheat even when you are not being watched? Is it known that you will honor God even in the little things—never trying to stretch your lunch-hour limit or taking an extra ten minutes at a coffee break or stealing in some other way because your job allows you certain freedoms?

How difficult it is to want to give people the liberty to develop and grow and then see them use that liberty to do the opposite—not work, not develop, not grow. It hurts to see it at the employer-employee level, but how much more it must hurt God to see Christians abusing the liberties they have in their new life in Christ. What a painful thing it is when a Christian will do less, not more, or abuse people because of his freedom in Christ.

Can God trust you to follow him even when some in the Church may not fully understand what your obedience means? Can he trust you to do what is right whether or not it comes out well by human standards, that you will do it because you are convinced that he has called you to do so which is the only reason you need?

Can God trust you to give away the love that he has given to you and to do it with abandonment? Can he trust you to hold on to him tightly in temptation and seek the way of escape that he provides? Can he trust you to know what you can and cannot do in Christ, and yet trust you not to judge others who have no restraints because they don't have Christ?

Can you be trusted to avoid the appearance of evil for the kingdom's sake and yet not avoid a potentially dangerous situation if it means helping, rescuing, delivering an unbeliever or strengthening some brother or sister in Christ?

There are biblical rules that we must obey before God. But we can't judge others who do not obey those rules. For example, I do not, when I have control of my circumstances, ever work on Sunday. I may work long hours six days a week, but Sunday is a day of rest. It is the Lord's day. It is for worship, and I need that time of worship. Therefore I will not make others work by shopping in stores or eating in restaurants or even buying gasoline if I can in any way avoid it. And yet I try not to be legalistic about it, for some Christians do it and before God have peace as they do it. I have not even kept my teenaged children from working on Sunday afternoons. In fact, I know that many of those they serve are Christians who use Sunday for pleasure and family business.

And I have helped my neighbors on Sunday to do things that I would never do for myself. Occasionally that has turned out to be a witness because they know from my lifestyle that I do not do those things for myself on Sunday.

Here is another example: I believe strongly that divorce and remarriage is wrong. I cannot accept it on the basis of Scripture. I believe a vow is a vow, that a union is a union, and that it cannot be broken. And I weep over those who look for escape from marriage on the basis that "God wants me to be happy." I will work for healing and can point to homes today where everything was against that marriage and yet it has held and the couple is growing and deepening in their love for each other and in their faith because they refused to divorce. Yet I can love and care for those who do not hold that view and have gone against what I consider to be the strong will of God. I can love them no less. If anything, I have despised my own failure to help them earlier when perhaps something might have been done. I have prayed for and loved people after they have divorced and later when they have found new partners. But my beliefs are the same about the biblical basis for staying together.

Some will charge, "You condemn in silence." But on two occasions I have performed the weddings of divorced people; they knew my stand but they also knew that I loved them. Some don't understand this "contradiction." It is simply that vows are vows, but healing is important too.

Or another example: I believe in tithing on my gross income not my net income. I believe that tithe money is not mine and can't be spent in any way, not even to pay my taxes. The money is God's and true giving on my part does not even begin until the tithe has first been given.to him. I believe that if I hold back any part of the full 10 percent saying, "That belongs to the government," or, "This is mine" it is stealing. The first 10 percent of the gross is his.

And yet I cannot feel self-righteous or condemn those who do not practice that. I must do what I must do before God—that is a rule for me to follow, not a rule for measuring others.

I believe in a daily prayer time alone with God, and

that it must be kept faithfully. Yet I know many who cannot and do not keep such a time. It is not mine to judge them, because my responsibility before God is for myself. Other people must do as they honestly will before God. They are his too, and I will not play God. Yet I will help others in all the ways I can if I am asked to help them establish a quiet time. I will try to be trustworthy enough to live out what I say I believe.

We are to be light. We are to be life "offerers." We are to be faithful in proclaiming and practicing the truth that Jesus came to reveal. We must do nothing less than our best for people and for God. And, because we are in him and because we are secure and because we vow to be faithful, we can do our best— for he is in us.

Can you be trusted? Can you really be trusted? Does God know it? Do your friends know it? Do even strangers know it?

I once wrote an article about discipline and received some interesting responses. A few came from those who agreed with me, but some responses were from those who didn't. To them discipline looked like a form of works, not faith. They argued that if I really trusted Christ, if I was really a believer, I would have no rules. F. P. Harton said: "Self-discipline is greatly assisted by the making and keeping of a wise Rule of Life. To the novice this sounds a very forbidding and complicated thing, but it should be neither. The soul that tries to live without rule never really forms habits of virtue or learns to live the Christian life as it should; for without rule the whole of the conduct of life depends on the whim of the moment, instead of being regulated with regard to the will of God, and

149

the soul never knows for certain what to do next." It takes faith to be disciplined. Only in faith can one be disciplined or discipline himself. Only when someone trusts God can he be trustworthy before God. James said, "Faith without works is dead" (James 2:26, KJV).

You can have faith and works together—you can be alive and trustworthy. God wants that for you. Because you are trusted, look at all that you have from God. You have gifts to give away.

# TEN
# Love Giver

† *Simon, Son of Jonas, lovest thou me more than these? He saith unto him, Yea, Lord; thou knowest that I love thee . . . . Feed my lambs* [John 21:15, KJV].

It follows—when I can be trusted, then I can be a love giver. Why? Because I am free by God and for God. "If the Son therefore shall make you free, ye shall be free indeed" (John 8:36, KJV). He has freed me from all that once limited me, and I am now liberated to be all that he designed me to be. I belong to the Giving One who gave himself for me and continually gives himself. Because of him I have become a "giveaway."

When I first moved to West Virginia as a young minister, it took me awhile to become accustomed to mountain ways. One afternoon I went calling with a deacon of the little church that I pastored. We drove down a narrow, winding dirt road back into one of the hollows and stopped at a little clearing where a cabin stood. Dogs growled at us as we got out of the car; chickens scattered as we approached the wooden steps to the door. A grizzled man greeted us with a look of suspicion. He had lived all his life in those hills and wasn't used to having townspeople come back that far into the hollows. He was a self-taught, homespun philosopher, an independent type, characteristic of mountain people. Besides scratching out a little garden for his sustenance, he was a gun trader. We had come to talk to him about his need for Jesus Christ.

He had heard the "Christian pitch" before and in his slow drawl kept me, a young, eager preacher, somewhat off balance; I was certainly not in control. After we had talked for about an hour he said, "Preacher, you got a gun?"

I replied, "No, I don't."

"I'm going to give you one," he said, and walked over to the wall where various guns were leaning. He picked up a 16-gauge shotgun, stuck it in my hand, and said gruffly, "Take it."

I started to argue, "But I can't take this gun, this is your livelihood. You trade these. I'll buy a gun for hunting someday, but, no, I can't take this."

"Don't you want that gun?" he accused, and then before I could finish stuttering my refusal, he stomped into the kitchen.

Quickly the deacon with me leaned over and in a commanding whisper said, "Take the gun!" Then, before I could protest, the gun trader stepped back into the room.

But I had caught that deacon's urgency and said, "I'm really pleased that you want me to have the shotgun. I've never received a gift like this before. I don't know how to thank you. You are a very generous man." And then I told him how I looked forward to rabbit hunting season. He didn't smile, but I could tell he was pleased.

As we drove back to town, the deacon said, "Preacher, don't you understand? You want to give him the gospel, but if you did he would be taking something from you. First you have to take something from him. Now, when you see him again, you will be indebted to him and he will listen to you."

I learned something that day about giving. Sometimes the first gift a Christian can give is to take.

But that doesn't mean we always have to receive before we give. Most of the time we give ourselves as well as our message without receiving anything—ever.

The liberation of obedience, the liberation from materialism, the liberation of discipleship free me. The things that once kept me hesitant and reserved now no longer matter. People's put-downs, fear that the criticism of my ideas is a criticism of me, fear of upmanship by someone else are things I need not be afraid of anymore. I was chosen before the foundation of the world (Ephesians 1:4). I am special to God. Therefore I can offer myself and I must offer myself as a gift to the body of Christ and to those who do not believe in Christ, even to those who hate him.

Within the church, I am a part of the body. I know that there are gifts that God has given to me which he will develop. Those are his gifts, but they are mine to exercise. As I use them I make a present of them to other members of the body. God made me the way I am so that I can do that. He crafted me for that, equipped me for that, and indeed expects me to strengthen others in the body with "my" gifts even as others strengthen me with theirs.

We are gift givers to and for one another, not for our sake but for his sake and for the sake of the body. We do it quietly, without attracting attention to ourselves. We stay out of the way. George Laird Hunt says, "The word minister means servant, servant of God, and he serves best who attracts little attention to himself and simply lets his Master work."

Filled by the ever-present Holy Spirit, each member of the body gives himself to other members as God puts them together. And together they perform a ministry as God intended it to be performed. We do not have to measure the effect of that ministry ourselves, although certainly we are aware of the effects. God measures by his standard. We don't have to analyze where each step of obedience is leading, how each gift applies, or be shown personally how we fulfill his role for us, though we are to be wise and worshipful about it when we are shown. We serve and give, and that is a completely satisfying way to live.

There is freedom in this kind of living because we know that he has us in his will. We are participants with God in his purpose and plan even though we may or may not know exactly how we are participating. In that participation, we receive what God is and give what God is. Because we are loved, we love. We are love givers. We are not foolish with it, for love is an active, thoughtful gift—God's gift through us, a strong divine love, not a weak, insipid, human love. We just do as we are—we love and we do it prayerfully. If we don't love that way we will forever be measuring love and lose out, grasping at "successes," crying over "failures," analyzing "developments" and "delays"—and in looking at the details, miss the larger picture, God's picture.

Being "love givers," we are quiet and we are content. The Word of God is correct: "In quietness and in confidence shall be your strength" (Isaiah, 30:15, KJV). We have time to listen, we have time to pray, we have time to teach, we have time for disciple-making, and we have time to bless and be blessed. Why? Because our time is not our own and our confidence is not in ourselves.

We can give ourselves both to believers and to unbelievers, and in giving ourselves be praying that we may bring them to God, which is the finest thing we can do for anyone. William Law said, "There is nothing that makes us love a man so much as praying for him; and when you can once do this sincerely for any man, you have fitted your soul for the performance of every thing that is kind and civil towards him."

We are proclaimers, both by our words and by our actions. What we proclaim, we proclaim with our being and our words—both coming out of the love of God. This is the greatest love and the greatest good. We are, as Jesus was, both the teacher and the content of the teaching.

And, as Jesus who came to the world, we will not limit what we give in his name or what we are by his power only to those who are "our own kind." He came to the world, so we go to the world too.

There was a time when I believed so strongly in separation from unbelievers that it was hard for me to live the love of God before an unbeliever, especially if he was a clergyman who denied the basic tenets of the Christian faith. Then, during a year-long course in clinical counseling, I saw myself mirrored in a fellow student. In this person's negative ways and attitudes I saw myself and I learned about being a love giver. This young clergyman, who was very much like me in his theological stance, was asked, "Do you love that man?" referring to a fellow clergyman who had belittled his fundamentalist beliefs.

"Yes, the Bible tells me to."

"But do you love him?"

"Yes, because Jesus does."

As I listened to him I heard what I was saying. I, too, could "love" because "loving" was what I was supposed to do—which was in fact no love at all. I learned from hearing my colleague mouth phrases without opening his heart in love that my "biblical" love was neither biblical nor love.

Love is love that is inside and comes out. It is not "love if," or "love because," but *love*—it cannot be synthetic. It touches everything we do and every person we encounter. God is love and there is no shortage of his love in me when he has me. And because he has me, I neither generate his love nor conserve my energies in presenting it to others. I am free to be a love giver in whatever state or condition or place I am. That is freedom. Love frees.

Our freedom in Christ is the freedom to follow the dictates of Jesus who himself could work long hours or leave everything and go alone to pray (Mark 1:35). Jesus, the Divine Son of God, showed both the "what" of the Father's love and the "how" of it.

Jesus had a purpose; it is described for us in the Gospels. We have a purpose too. We are to follow him. Jesus came for a reason; we're here for a reason too—we are love givers.

To be in Christ is to have the same ministry that Jesus referred to when he took the prophet's words and said, "The Spirit of the Lord is upon me, because he hath anointed me to preach the gospel to the poor; he hath sent me to heal the brokenhearted, to preach deliverance to the captives, and recovering of sight to the blind, to set at liberty them that are bruised, to preach the acceptable year of the Lord" (Luke 4:18, 19, KJV).

To be his is to move easily and quietly within the world and within the Church, not straining, not struggling, not trying to become, because we already are in him and our becoming is within that framework of his life.

In ministry, in evangelism, in all of life, we have the time and the love to reach out, for both time and love are God's and are of his giving. He knows best how to utilize each day and each situation so that we can love; we need not worry about "redeeming the time." In him, mine is the freedom to work many hours a day or the freedom sometimes not to work at all, simply to rest and enjoy life. It is the freedom to give myself away until I am exhausted—or to go fishing to restore my body and soul.

There is a wholeness to all of this. It is the wholeness of understanding who I am, in coming to love my neighbor as myself, in coming to appreciate the gifts that God has given to me—the gifts that I can give away. It's the discovery of pleasure with myself. I can truly appreciate me because I am loved and appreciated by God. And with that sense of personal value, I have also the awareness that in Christ I have so much to give away. It is given in humility, both to the Church and to the world, because I have so much and because none of it is of my own making. It comes from obedience and works itself out in obedience. George Laird Hunt says, "Humility is not a technique with which the adroit leader wins friends and influences people. It is the essential mark of obedience, the attitude of the person who knows that he is reconciled to God by a deed of God, and that the grace of God equips him for the service he is called to render to the community and the world."

No one gives a cheap gift if he truly means to do something special for somebody. He gives a good gift. That's what the Christian is—a good gift. How foolish it is for a Christian, having been saved by grace and knowing the complete work that Jesus did in him to make him righteous, to think that he can then add to that righteousness by his own efforts or settle for less than God supplies. Rather, the Christian lives and moves and has his being in him, the One who fulfills his righteousness within us, the One who sends us into communities as his gifts, bearing the truth, the love, the redeeming plan of God to our Judeas, our Samarias, and to the uttermost parts of our earth.

This is why a Christian can keep a low profile but still get into other people's hearts, winning them to the highest and the best. In Jesus, the Christian can change the hardened structures around him. The Christian who is secure in Jesus does not have identity problems or ego needs. He doesn't have to be watching to see if the right people are recognizing him and what he is doing. There is only one "audience" for the Christian—the One he loves, the Lord himself.

William Law said, "Every good thought that we have, every good action that we do, lays us open to pride, and exposes us to the assaults of vanity and self-satisfaction." A Christian leader, noting the difference between the effective Christians and the noisy, incompetent ones, said, "Did you ever notice how ego and incompetence usually go together?"

We can do so much and be so much if our reason for doing what we do and giving what we give is

Jesus. I know a man who realized several years ago that just earning a paycheck wasn't all that God put him on this earth to do. He left an important position to put his efforts into Christian ministry. Ten years later he was nowhere near to earning the salary that he had in his previous position but, as he put it, "My wife and I are nearer the Lord, and we don't lack for anything." He will never make the headlines. No one knows very much about him—except God.

Some years ago in Germany a theologian and pastor named Augusta Hermann Franke established an orphanage. He didn't intend to start one, but while supporting the beggar children who came to his door he also taught them the Scriptures. Then when he opened his home to one orphan boy, he found that there were other brothers and sisters too. So he took them all. By the time Franke died he had built an orphanage, a primary and secondary school, a hospital, and a home for the aged. His little project of caring for the children at his door had developed into a major work.

As Franke asked others for help in supporting his homes, he learned that it was mostly the poor, not the rich, who gave to help others. The rich kept what they had or gave only a pittance. It was with money from the poor that he helped the orphan children and the aged. It is often that way today, too.

The disciple, not being his own, has everything to give. Because he belongs to the One who gave himself, his nature is giving; it cannot be any other way. He is a Christian. He has the desires of the One who lives in him. Jesus did not clutch or grasp at his place with the Father but left it to give himself for us. We receivers of that gift are givers too. We desire to help others. It is as incongruous to hear someone give a testimony about being in Christ while ignoring others in need as it is for the unsaved to give a testimony about being redeemed. Those who love Jesus care for those for whom Jesus cared. "Lord, when saw we thee an hungered, and fed thee? or thirsty, and gave thee drink? When saw we thee a stranger, and took thee in? or naked, and clothed thee? Or when saw we thee sick, or in prison, and came unto thee? And the King shall answer and say unto them, Verily I say unto you, Inasmuch as ye have done it unto one of the least of these my brethren, ye have done it unto me" (Matthew 25:37–40, KJV).

When God leads someone across our paths, whether for a few minutes or a few days, we give him what he needs. We care, minister, and instruct because God has placed them with us and us with them.

In his book about Justo Gonzalez, Floyd Shacklock tells about a man in Santiago, Chile, who was arrested by the police for being drunk. On the way to the jail, two Christian men asked the police if they would give the man to them to take care of. The police did. The men fed him, cared for him, found him a job, and told him about Jesus. The writer tells us, "The gospel meant a new life for Munoz. He began to repair shoes and was able to make a simple living for his family. He began to talk to his neighbors about the love of God that was changing his life. Step by step he found himself: sober, employed and industrious; soon he was leading a group of neighbors in worship.

"It was not easy to be their leader, for he could not read. He had to memorize the Bible verses that his wife read to him. He explained the verses to his

friends in terms of their daily lives and hungers. Before long he became the pastor of a new congregation
of seventy members and had 150 children in a Sunday
school. He still made his living as a shoemaker."

Are you available to give as those two Christian
men gave? People are desperate for care and they are
hungry for God. They need a chance to see God in
you, and to feel the power and warmth of God from
you. You are their window.

Who in the world has access to you? Who knows
that you live for God and are available to them? Do
you communicate peace or do you communicate busy-
ness? Is there ever time for people who need help to
reach you? If not, then maybe there isn't even time for
God to reach you either.

Whose life is better because you are here on this
earth, because you live where you live and know
whom you know and do what you do? What good
are you for someone else?

For example, who is reaching out in a personal,
genuine way to the international students on the university campus near you? They wonder when they
are invited once for dinner, "ministered to," and then
dropped, not to be invited again. They don't understand when people say, "How are you?" but imply in
walking away that they don't really care or want to
know. They don't know what to do with shallow
friendships which don't go anywhere. Do you know
even one person from another country or culture? Do
you love them?

During the Billy Graham Cambridge Mission in
1980, I met a man named Vijay Menon. He came to
Christ out of Hinduism, but he had to find Christ on
his own; no one helped him. Today, realizing the

161

value of Christian friendship, he has a mission to international people in London where he works as a Class A engineer; and he goes annually to university student missions where he serves on his own time.

With a glow of love, he told me about the students to whom he ministers. He told me where each one of them was spiritually and which step they had taken toward Christ. Each was as special to him as his own family. He is a love giver. He cares.

At Oxford, I spent a Saturday morning having coffee with a student who called himself "an indifferent agnostic." He wanted to talk about Jesus. He was eager to learn what it was that so satisfied me in Christ. Even though he claimed indifference, he pursued this conversation. He needed to know and talk to a Christian. People like him are everywhere.

One afternoon, after talking to two Irish students at Cambridge, I started to leave for another appointment. They ran after me to invite me to their rooms for tea. They wanted to know more about personal faith in Christ. People are searching, and many of us aren't even aware of it because we haven't opened the way for them to express themselves. We haven't even shown cursory interest. We need to help them along on the road to determining that they could have God in their lives too.

Several years ago a Danish schoolteacher came to live with our family. She was in the United States for twenty-four weeks, twelve of them with us, while taking graduate studies in education at Rutgers University. We were far apart biblically and socially. She believed that her son should live with various women before marriage or else "how would he know whom he wanted to marry?" She challenged us when we spanked one of our children. She never sought our Christ. Were those twelve weeks a waste of our time? Should we have given her a quick plan of salvation and then ignored her if she didn't respond, going after better "pickings?" Since we couldn't point to "success" with her, did we fail God? We did what we felt we should do. We entrusted both our witness and her response to God. For twelve weeks we were the ones to be her "Christians." We could only give what we had. Now we can only trust.

Who is reaching out to the children around you? The ones who need a foster parent or a big brother or sister? There are fewer and fewer two-parent homes now and there is a desperate need for love and adult role models. Fatherless children need to relate to a man. Motherless children need a "mom" to talk to. Is your home open to these children? You have more than yourself to give; you have the gifts that God has given to you to offer to someone else. If you could love just one: affirm him, help him, teach him—just one. Even if you never saw the results in your life-time, you would be praying and you would be loving. God would honor that.

Cameron V. Thompson of "Back to the Bible," explains, "Our prayers should be persistent. God's delays are not denials. Each day brings the answers to our prayers nearer. . . . At a meeting in a small town in the United States a very old man was converted. Another old man stepped forward and with tears told how fifty years earlier twenty-five young people had made a pledge to pray for this man every day. Said he, 'I am the only one still living to see the prayers of fifty years answered.' "

You may never know what you do when you act

in love. It doesn't matter—just reach out in love anyway.

Who is touching the lives of the deserted elderly? The people alone in small inner-city apartments or unvisited in nursing homes? One young couple I know spends every Sunday afternoon visiting people in a retirement home. They choose Sunday because that's when those who have families get their visitors, but the ones without families feel the most lonely. This young couple offers themselves. They are "surrogate children." Each week they listen to the same stories that they heard the week before, look at the same photographs that they have seen many times, but they don't mind because they are love givers—people who give themselves and give their love. Jesus would have them do that.

Who is writing letters for those in hospitals or nursing homes who are too weak to write? I know a woman in her eighties who has given more than 4,000 hours of volunteer work to patients in hospitals. She keeps giving and she is happy. I know another woman who is ten years younger but is miserable because she says, "No one ever does anything for me." There is health in being a love giver. Who can best express the love of Jesus? Not the one who has his thoughts on his own personal wants; only the love giver can do it because his time and life and love are not his own.

And when people start to give in one area, it affects the other areas of their lives too. I have a friend who is a listener. She works as a receptionist in a doctor's office. People come seeking treatment for physical ailments, but while they are waiting to see the doctor some of them talk to her, spilling out their anxieties about family or future. She isn't trying to be a doctor, but she knows that part of their treatment is occurring right there, in the outer office, as she listens. She is a different kind of physician, but she is a physician.

Who is going to the jails and prisons to minister there? When I was a young minister I went every week to a medium security prison in Virginia about sixty miles from my home. I came to know about a dozen inmates quite well. I was allowed to eat lunch with them and talk and listen. At first they all talked about being innocent, about being there through no fault of their own. But then the talk of their innocence passed and they got honest, talking about themselves, their feelings, their fears. Soon I was picking up on biblical subjects one week right where I had left off the week before—the continuity was coming with their feelings of security with me.

One day one of the men opened his heart and soul to Jesus Christ, accepting him as Savior and Lord. Shortly after that I moved to another state and lost contact with those men. But about a year later the inmate who had accepted Christ showed up at my church study, suitcase in hand. I heard a knock on my door, and when I opened the door there he stood. He was out, he said; had served his full sentence rather than take an early parole because he had nowhere to go to start life again and wanted to leave the state to come to me. I took this ex-convict home and he moved in with us. We found him a job and kept him until he had a little money of his own, then helped him find a small apartment.

That was nearly twenty years ago, and I haven't seen him since. As far as I know he still lives in that community. I know that he is married and is involved in a church. He was, as far as I know, the only one who came to Christ from more than a year of visits, but I would have gone to that prison even if there had been none. People need us—as Christians we *have* to give.

But that doesn't mean that we are only responders to need; love givers are initiators. They are among the most disciplined people anywhere. The time for giving has to come out of the same twenty-four-hour day that everyone else has, and that time is precious. There are always more people with needs than there is time to give, and we have to decide prayerfully how to give ourselves to the people who have the most urgent needs. And the time given has to be *quality* time—we can't rush from one person to another like a politician shaking hands on the campaign trail. I've learned a lot about giving from watching other people. Sometimes one experience teaches two lessons.

I remember watching a clergyman who measured his effectiveness by the number of calls he made in a day. In the little town where I lived there was a small hospital, and since everyone knew everyone else, several clergy often visited the same patients.

One day, sitting by a patient's bedside, I looked up as this minister rushed breathlessly into the room. He asked the patient, "How are you?" and then, without waiting for an answer, talked about God, read a passage of Scripture, said, "Let's pray," and fled. The patient hadn't had time to respond at all. Later I learned that several patients had requested that the clergyman not be allowed into their rooms; the flurry of his visits caused emotional strain.

So, seeing how he acted and thinking I knew more than he did, I decided to do the opposite—just be quiet—which was also wrong. One day a man I knew was admitted to the hospital suffering injuries from a car crash. He was a hard drinker; his reputation in town was that of a tough-living individual who was unapproachable with the gospel. So no one tried to reach him, including me.

I visited him because his wife asked me to, and I practiced my "I-won't-be-like-that-other-clergy-man" routine. I said nothing about Christ. Then, after a few minutes with him, preparing to leave, I said casually, "Well, if there is ever anything I can do for you, let me know," and started to walk out the door. As I reached the door he called out. I turned and saw tears streaming down his face. With a choking voice he said, "Please, I want to be saved."

Had I been like Jesus I would have been sensitive—to listen, to ask, to initiate, to respond. I almost missed God's opportunity in that hospital room. I might have gone on for years, never knowing what I'd done, repeating that act again and again. I learned that day that just as we can be overbearing and insensitive, we can also be insensitive in our efforts not to be overbearing.

The French philosopher Emile Cailliet said, "The man of power, then, is the Christ-like man—shall I say it—the saint. And let there be no mistake about it, the saint is the truly successful man. It is not only that his life naturally issues in an ever-faithful, ever watchful obedience. Faithfulness and watchfulness are so natural to him that his obedience never gives the impression of effort, still less of strain. It is visibly God in him who does what he does."

It is easy to be consumed by people when you are a love giver. If that happens, you can lose your usefulness. In fact, you may start to become irritated because someone is consuming so much of your time; you may even become angry at yourself because you let that person do so. When others are permitted to take from you and drain you, the "love" does them little good. Parents aren't better parents when they give in to every cry of their child. They decide what the child needs and lovingly give their attention to that need. They give because they love the child; they withhold because they love the child. They can't give what is really needed if they are always running to do whatever the child demands. So it is with us as Jesus' love givers.

I have learned that often the same people who keep returning for help are not helped nor do they always want to be helped. Years ago it dawned on me that I was giving the same few people most of my time, with little result. My willingness to come every time they called was not doing them any favors at all. So I began to hold back. I learned that I had to determine prayerfully their needs for them. Otherwise I became exhausted or, worse, I became angry, even bitter. Those who have needs also need to struggle some on their own. It's the only way they can learn. Sometimes love means letting them alone in their pain. This sounds cruel but it isn't, for we must give, not be used. It sounds as if we "determine" the needs of others. No, at least not at first. We give without question, but when we see that all the giving is to the same person or persons, we must judge our giving and their taking. Withholding for awhile might be the better gift.

One day a man came to my house for counselling. He didn't know what he wanted and couldn't even express what he felt. I was available to him then and for several succeeding visits, but only within limits or I would have never been available to anybody else. I determined when I would see him next. I didn't let him dictate. And because I would not let him consume my time, he learned to vocalize his needs and to wrestle with some of his problems himself—he had to. It was for him a profitable "withholding."

A caution needs to be given here about the act of caring. Some Christians are so insecure that they must be "needed" by others all the time. There are many exhausted Christians running around, pleased with themselves at how much they are giving to others yet hurting inside at the same time. They are quick to tell everybody how busy they are, how great are the demands upon them. But when others step in to take some of the pressures off them, they become resentful. They are really not givers but takers, needing people to need them. It is a backward offering.

These are the people who resent others who "don't give as much as I do" yet continue to take all they can on themselves, even to the detriment of family and personal health. They have to have that tired, "I'm-serving-Jesus" look. This is very sad because they are serving themselves and calling it "serving Christ," running themselves down physically and emotionally, and bringing no honor to Christ who is their Lord. They are not ministering in Christ and for Christ but for their own satisfaction and their own ego needs. They are not helping others; they are impressing themselves and anyone who might notice "how helpful I am."

Why do we think that God is pleased with us when we are worn out? Usually these exhausted love givers can never be questioned about what they are doing; they see their anxiety as Christian responsibility, and they are very virtuous about it, never understanding that they might trust Christ to use *others* as well.

God knows who we are and what we have to offer because he gave us our gifts. And he gave others their gifts too. We cheat others in the body when we insist on doing everything ourselves. Learn to be content to "change the dressings" so that healing can come. Don't try to force healing so that people can see what a good physician you are. You aren't *the* Physician.

We are to be like an instrument in the musician's hand. We don't try to see how loudly we can play, but play the best we can as he chooses to use us, not all the time, but when it's our turn. We know that we are only one part of the whole orchestra. Those who follow the Conductor are part of a divine symphony. Those who do not, contribute to cacophony.

Love givers always have the problem of personal anxiety. We can't reach enough people. We always see more needs. We feel that there are never enough hours or years. But that's where discipleship comes in. We will always have the weak and the sick and the poor with us. Jesus told us we would. He is our example. He didn't panic about it. He could be content with healing some, feeding some, because his will was to do the Father's will. When people were pressing in around him, he said, "I have others, too." And sometimes he left them. It's not wrong to leave. It isn't wrong to want to be alone. Jesus did it. We need time to pray in order to have something more to give the next time. Christians, of all people, should know that. They have to have love to give love. They have to go to the well.

Jesus responded to people selectively. He called out the blind man and the cripple. He determined their needs and touched them. He gave himself away, but always as the One whose will was to do the will of "him who sent me." And that is our rule too.

If you aren't giving, you're like the Dead Sea—closed up. The true follower of Jesus is a love giver whose life is full and overflowing. He is a fresh, flowing stream, the conduit of Jesus Christ who is himself the well of Living Water.

And having found the way to give without struggle or anxiety, the Christian disciple—the friend of God—finds that being in Christ, used by Christ, blessed of Christ, he has in fact what is available to every person who wants it—inner peace.

# The Way to Inner Peace

† *And the peace of God, which passeth all understanding, shall keep your hearts and minds through Christ Jesus* [Philippians 4:7, KJV].

One snowy afternoon when Andrea and I were out shopping together, I darted across the street in front of oncoming traffic thinking that she was right behind me. But when I turned around to look, she was still standing on the opposite curb waiting for a break in the traffic. When she finally crossed, I asked, "Why didn't you come with me?"

Matter-of-factly she replied, "Because I'm a klutz; I have to allow time to fall down and get back up and still make it across the street before a car hits me." That was it, straight out, no embarrassment or apology. And I felt a warm response at how special she is. She is so honest.

What security others have within! I'm not that way. I couldn't say something like that. Maybe it's in my genes, maybe I am a worrier, or maybe I have a sense of inadequacy. I don't roll with changes or slough off problems. I tend to get nervous, bound-up emotionally.

I even have a poor sense of direction. I can get lost

faster than anybody I know. My children still smile, even though they should be used to it by now, at how I turn down the wrong street to get to our house, or pull on a door handle clearly labeled "push." Sometimes I think I accomplish what I accomplish only through long hours of hard work, doing something incorrectly several times, until inevitably I discover how to do it right.

God must smile a lot at my inept struggles. He is near as I stumble along, but it took me awhile before I found peace in that.

When I was a young minister, newly ordained, I was so nervous about Sunday mornings that my stomach would become upset. And when I made mistakes—well, I still remember my first Easter sermon. When I saw the size of that congregation, people whom I had never seen in church before, I was even more nervous than usual. I tried to remember the instructions of my seminary homiletics professor: "Memorize your first words; the rest will follow." So, while the choir was singing the Easter anthem, I kept repeating to myself the opening sentence of my sermon, the words of the angel: "He is not here; he is risen." Over and over again, under my breath, I repeated that statement, "He is not here; he is risen." The choir stopped singing. I stood to my feet, strode to the pulpit, and in my loudest voice announced to the congregation, "He is not risen; he is here!" Then I simply stopped and stood there because I didn't know what to do next. Somehow, sputtering and stumbling, I got through the rest of the sermon.

I wanted to hide. But still, God used it. The congregation seemed to be listening even more intently, probably to hear what other blunders I was going to make, not wanting to miss any of the mistakes. They enjoyed it and that night many more people than usual turned out for the evening service, perhaps still chuckling. Yet it was an opportunity, so I took it, discarding the planned evening message and preaching on the text, "If He is not risen, we are without hope," using the morning mistake as my introduction.

Did I learn to relax from that? No! For the next two years I was still so nervous that I had to take stomach medication before preaching. I wanted to preach so well that I was getting in my own way. I was not learning how to trust the One who had called me to preach; I was trusting myself. I could preach about the gifts of God, including his peace, but inner peace escaped me. I had to learn to seek it.

It wasn't until several years later, when a returned missionary saw my problem and prayed for me and my emotions, that I was helped to see that the One whom I was trusting for eternal peace was also the One who offered daily peace. Jesus said, "My peace I give unto you; not as the world giveth, give I unto you" (John 14:27, KJV). And he keeps that promise. This didn't eliminate my mistakes, but I began to see that I could make mistakes and still have his peace.

Seeking peace sent me to the Scriptures. I've had to do that because given any difficult situation I too readily run back to depending upon myself. I need the promises of God.

It is the appropriation of God's promises that has helped me to have inner peace. For the One who bought me for eternity certainly holds me now. I don't have to find peace in what others think; I don't have to impress people. I've learned that I can't impress them anyway. I can't impress people with my talents or my skills or my wisdom or my repartee or my put-on *savoir faire*. I've learned that slowly, but I've learned.

One morning, shortly after I joined the Billy Graham Team, Andrea and I were having breakfast in a hotel when Ruth Graham joined us at our table. We had not met before and I certainly wanted to make a good impression. After awhile I could see that I was doing very well because she was gracious and warm, and by the time breakfast was over I was glowing. At least I was glowing until I got back to our room and glanced in the mirror. Stuck to the side of my nose was a piece of scrambled egg.

There is a way to inner peace but it isn't through our own sophistication, abilities, talents, or internal make-up; it is through God. Knowing that, I have to make an all-out determination to seek him, to obey him, and to appropriate all that he is and gives. G. Steinberger says, "We find peace in the same degree that we follow Him. And we retain it as long as we are one with Him. This peace is not something we must strive or pray for; it is given to us as soon as we take His yoke upon us and follow Him (Matthew 11:29)."

I have to follow him. I have to wait on him. I have to come to him and want him and trust him and then move on in his strength. Then, and only then, can I have the peace and assurance that all is well. And, having found that peace, I can delight in it.

Some people delight in personal progress, social gains, accumulation of things, the pleasure of accomplishment. I've learned that my delight comes from him or it doesn't come at all.

God wants to give his peace. He is the Peacegiver. It is his nature to give it. Inner peace comes to me not because I merit it but because he wants me to have it. That's not something that I have to hope is true or somehow convince myself is true. It is something that he is trying to convince me is true and so, being convinced by him, I take it. It's because of the peace he gives that I can move around in this world and function and take risks and take responsibility and make decisions and make mistakes.

Hannah Whitall Smith, who wrote *The Christian's Secret of a Happy Life,* said, "I believe God has made me a pioneer, so that I do not expect much sympathy and understanding as I go along; and the breaking through of hedges, and fences, and stone walls is not a very pleasant path. . . . But it is my nature. I cannot help it." No wonder she could talk about the happy life.

And Thomas Kelly, the Quaker, expressed the way I feel: "The basic response of the soul to the light is internal adoration and joy, thanksgiving and worship, self-surrender and listening. The secret places of the heart cease to be our noisy workshop. They become a holy sanctuary of adoration and of self-oblation, where we are kept in perfect peace, if our minds be stayed on Him who has found us in the inward springs of our life. And in brief intervals of over-powering visitation we are able to carry the sanctuary frame of mind out into the world, into its turmoil and its fitfulness, and in a hyperaesthesia of the soul, we see all mankind tinged with deeper shadows, and touched with Galilean glories. Powerfully are the springs of our will moved to an abandon of singing love toward God; powerfully are we moved

177

to a new and overcoming love toward time-blinded men and all creation. In this Center of Creation all things are ours, and we are Christ's and Christ is God's. We are owned men, ready to run and not be weary and walk and not faint." I have found that the true sanctuary of the soul comes not only in the quietness of my sanctuaries but even in the raucous marketplaces of life. The peace is his. It is in him, and he gives it.

I need to give my early mornings to prayer to have this peace. This is not a ritual—it's an absolute necessity. I would miss breakfast before I would miss my time of prayer. I cannot go into the world each day without having first enjoyed the sanctuary of the quiet time with God. If my day begins at 6:00, my inner clock says I have to be up at 5:00 or 5:15 at the latest. If I'm up all night on a long flight, I will spend part of it in prayer even if I am too sleepy to read Scripture. I run in fear—not a crippling fear but a healthy fear, a fear of not wanting to live apart from him and his guidance. And what comes from that is a deep peace, not because I have generated that peace through my activity but because he is God and he meets me. In any rough moment I can go back to him and say, "Lord, this morning I committed all of this to you. You promised to be with me." That helps, especially when difficult situations come.

There is no failure in the Lord. My mistakes might be just that—my mistakes. But there are no failures in him. He can and does correct my life's errors as long as I practice obedience, commitment, and trust.

And I have learned that there is peace even when things happen that are not of my doing, events or circumstances that come because I am a part of this decaying world. There is peace in the pain of illness, separation, loss, and failure. In my disappointments and frustrations, he is still God. He is my Rock, and I know he is there regardless of whether or not I sense him. Thomas Kelly said, "Don't be fooled by your sunny skies. When the rains descend and the floods come and the winds blow and beat upon your house, your private dwelling, your own family, your own fair hopes, your own strong muscles, your own body, your own soul itself, then it is well-nigh too late to build a house. You can only go inside what house you have and pray that it is founded upon the Rock. Be not deceived by distance in time or space, or the false security of a bank account and an automobile and good health and willing hands to work."

None of our ways or gathered things is going to guarantee peace. When all is gone, the peace is either there or it is not. It can't be manufactured. The house is either on the Rock or it is not. We either flee to the house we have or we get washed away.

There is comfort in knowing that it is God's enjoyment to give me his peace. It is God's enjoyment to hold me close to himself. It is God's pleasure to satisfy me and walk with me. It is his intention not to leave me or forsake me. That is not a realization we all come to quickly, but come to it we must. In his book *The Legacy of Bunyan,* the Reverend W. Y. Fullerton said, "Rabbi Duncan, that modest but eccentric saint of Edinburgh, in one of the melancholy moods which occasionally overtook him, thinking himself unworthy of God's salvation, began to croon a lullaby of Scripture texts in the original language, which was as familiar as his own; and all of the texts he murmured to himself contained the word 'grace.' Suddenly it struck him; 'Why the word "grace" means joy.' Shall I deny God His joy in refusing the joy He gives us by His grace?"

Will we do that? Will we deny God his joy? Look at what is ours on the whole broad avenue called inner peace. Look at the blessings and then learn to revel in them. Don't settle for your accomplishments or else that's all you will have. Don't be satisfied with your salary or else that's all you will have. Don't glory in your prestige or else that's all there will be. All of that is empty. Let God have his joy. Allow him the opportunity to enjoy giving himself and his gifts to you.

Look what comes from walking the road with him. Look at his promises! They are "beatitudes." They are his "blesseds" offered to us.

"Blessed are the poor in spirit," he said. Not the poor in money; they can be spiritually wealthy. Not the rich; they can be spiritually poor. But the poor in spirit. We are poor; we need to admit it. We need spiritual "handouts" from God. Those who are not spiritually wanting are the ones who will not be spiritually receiving. It is the poor in spirit that Jesus is talking about. The promise follows: "Theirs is the kingdom of heaven." This is not a someday-you-had-better-hope-it-will-be-yours kind of promise. It is a straight-out statement of fact—theirs is the kingdom of heaven. The poor in spirit are the kingdom receivers. They are God's kingdom dwellers. And in that kingdom, spiritual food comes not in snacks but in banquets.

"Blessed are they that mourn: for they shall be comforted" (Matthew 5:4, KJV). Just as the poor are not necessarily only the physically poor, neither are the mourners only those who lament the loss of a loved one. It is a deeper kind of mourning than that, just as poor in spirit is a deeper kind of poverty. It is a lament over sin. It is a lament over personal wickedness.

When we mourn like that we have God's assurance that we shall be comforted. We have his Word: "Thy sins be forgiven thee." Jesus does that. Scripture promises: "If we confess our sins, he is faithful and just to forgive us our sins, and to cleanse us from all unrighteousness" (1 John 1:9, KJV). Some people feel a little sorry for the consequences of their sin, the trouble it has caused them, but more than that is required for forgiveness. Forgiveness can come only when we confess our sins and turn from them. When we come to him as mourners, in deep sorrow over our spiritual condition, we shall be comforted. That is the gateway to peace. For, "he is able also to save them to the uttermost that come unto God by him" (Hebrews 7:25, KJV).

"Blessed are the meek." He doesn't say weak, but meek. Often the strongest people are the meekest. It takes a strong person to be meek, to be like Jesus, to be kissed by a traitor, to turn the other cheek. Believers who walk with Jesus can be strong like that— waiting, enduring, putting up with something, letting "patience have her perfect work, that ye may be perfect and entire, wanting nothing" (James 1:4, KJV). The blessed meek person is the humble one, the one who bows to God. The ungodly, the ones "too strong" to need God, will soon be swept away. When the end comes, they will be gone. God remains, and so do the meek who by God's act inherit the earth.

"Blessed are they which do hunger and thirst after righteousness." Be careful with this one. It is the hungering and thirsting for righteousness that Jesus calls "blessed"—it isn't eating or drinking. We usually call a person "blessed" when he has plenty to eat or drink or wear or use. But that's not what Jesus is saying.

We have all been hungry and thirsty, and when we are that's all that we can think about. Hunger and thirst overrule every other human desire. We don't want to do anything or go anywhere or have anything until that hunger and thirst is satisfied. It is a passionate need—it controls us. It drives us.

What do you hunger for? Listen to the talk in a locker room, at an investors' meeting, or at your club. You can tell what people hunger and thirst for by the things they talk about. Their conversations reveal the appetites that drive them.

The psalmist said, "As the hart panteth after the water brooks, so panteth my soul after thee, O God" (Psalm 42:1, KJV). When we crave God and his righteousness more than we crave anything else, when to savor and delight in the righteousness of God is the only thing that will satisfy us, then that is what Jesus calls "blessed."

When we receive his righteousness and have the satisfaction of it, we will want that righteousness every day just as we want food and drink every day. And when we want Jesus Christ and his righteousness day after day, we will be satisfied. We won't be complacent, but we will be satisfied. For we will come to Christ craving his satisfying food and drink; he is himself that food and drink, and he does satisfy.

"Blessed are the merciful." God is a God of mercy; he proved that in giving his Son Jesus Christ on the cross. He proved it on Easter morning when he raised his Son from the dead. His followers, those who are really his, are merciful too. They can be no less nor do no less than the Master they call their own. The Christian will not say, "I'll get him!" or "Just wait; my turn will come!" He can't, he won't, because God is merciful. What God is, the Christian is. Being in him is the description of a believer. If people hear me claim his name, they have every right to expect me to be an example of what he is like.

And lest we forget, the model prayer that Jesus gave us includes the words, "And forgive us our debts [trespasses] as we forgive. . . ." In other words, we pray to be forgiven and we receive forgiveness to the same degree that we forgive others. We are asking for God's mercy in the same amount that we offer mercy to others. Some of us wouldn't pray that way if we knew what we were really asking of God. Some of us don't show much mercy. If God showed mercy to us only to the same degree that we show mercy to others, what would become of us?

Is God's mercy free? Then ours must be too. Does God first expect me to become better to receive mercy? Not at all. "While we were yet sinners, Christ died for us" (Romans 5:8, KJV). So there is to be no qualification to our mercy-giving either. We are to be as merciful as the Mercy Giver is merciful. "They shall obtain mercy" is not a trade-off policy, a tit-for-tat policy; it's a love policy.

"Blessed are the pure in heart." There is only One who is truly pure in heart—God. A pure heart is not ours by our own nature. Jeremiah said, "The heart is deceitful above all things, and desperately wicked: who can know it?" (Jeremiah 17:9, KJV). We need what God alone can give: "A new heart also will I give you, and a new spirit will I put within you: and I will take away the stony heart out of your flesh, and I will give you an heart of flesh" (Ezekiel 36:26, KJV).

In order to be pure like him, we have to be washed by him. That's why Jesus said, "If I wash thee not, thou hast no part with me" (John 13:8, KJV). He is the cleansing One. He examines our hearts with the searchlight of his own gaze. He is the One able to look into the corners (the "folds," Augustine called them) where the impurities collect. And he does the washing. That's what "pure" is; something with the impurities taken out.

When we are washed by him, cleansed in the heart, then we shall see God, for someday "we shall be like him; for we shall see him as he is" (1 John 3:2, KJV). That's a promise. "They shall see God" (Matthew 5:8, KJV). And not only later, in heaven, but now—every day. We will see God: we will see him now in the events of our lives, and we will see him someday face to face for all eternity.

The cleansing Savior is the fellowshipping Savior—we will be made clean and we will be with him; and the more intimate we are with him, the cleaner we will be. He makes us pure by virtue of his purity.

"Blessed are the peacemakers, for they shall be called the children of God." Only a son of God can be a peacemaker, for two reasons. A peacemaker is one who knows what peace is. A person cannot work for real peace if he doesn't understand real peace. Peace with God is the ultimate, final peace. It is more than a cessation of hostilities. It is more than a cease fire. It is a coming into harmonious relationship. That's what the follower of Jesus Christ has, a harmonious relationship made possible for him by the One called the

"Prince of Peace." The Christian can be a peacemaker because he knows real peace.

The other reason is that peacemakers are in the reconciling business. The follower of Jesus has been reconciled. He has been brought back into fellowship with God and is therefore able to be an extender of that reconciliation to all who are around him, to his whole world. Where he is, there is peace. How sad when a Christian is the sower of discord or dissension, causing strife instead of bringing warring parties together. God ended the war between us and brought us to himself in peace. We can be no less than bearers of that peace to others who are still at war with God and with their fellow man.

As sons of God who are able to use that wonderful personal word, "Abba" (Father), we are justified. "Therefore being justified by faith, we have peace with God through our Lord Jesus Christ" (Romans 5:1, KJV). And since that's what we have, we cannot give less than what we have to others.

The last beatitude (or "blessed") is, "Blessed are they which are persecuted for righteousness' sake: for theirs is the kingdom of heaven." That doesn't mean we will always be persecuted as part of our discipleship or that it is a necessary part of being blessed. It does mean that when "men shall revile you, and persecute you, and shall say all manner of evil against you falsely, for my sake" (Matthew 5:11, KJV), there will still be reason to rejoice and be glad because we know that our reward in heaven is great.

Jesus is not giving an invitation for persecution; he is giving his word of comfort, a promise for when we are persecuted. The faithful follower of Jesus doesn't look for persecution, but he can expect it when his honesty, his moral character, his obedience to God runs counter to what Satan's people practice. Faithful believers also know that the reward from God is great. A person can bear anything when he knows that.

We can expect suffering as God's people—not seek it or cause it, but expect it. It has always been that way: "For so persecuted they the prophets which were before you" (Matthew 5:12, KJV). We are not exempt. We should not expect to be. The prophets spoke what God told them to speak, and it was enough to infuriate people. Jesus came loving people and preaching the kingdom, and it was enough to send him to the cross. The disciples then and the disciples now are no different than their Master.

But watch out. There are Christians who do unkind things, and when their actions backfire they think they are being persecuted "for righteousness' sake." There are Christians who decide on their own terms what following Jesus means, and then get hurt by it. There are Christians who cheat, who hurt, who break the commandments, and claim the resulting trouble as persecution for "righteousness' sake." They serve their egos and reap the result. They do not care about other people and then assume the response they get for their attitude is because they are "Christians." Jesus was never obnoxious. Jesus didn't do offensive things. Jesus offended precisely because there was nothing offensive about him. If a Christian has bad manners, a nasty tongue, a critical attitude, an unloving nature, or disgusting habits, he cannot blame the reaction he gets on his Christian walk.

I remember meeting a man who had erected a

flashing neon sign on the roof of his house. All night long it flashed "Jesus Saves" on and off. When irate neighbors called the police to complain that they were being kept awake by that flashing light, the man wailed that he was being persecuted for righteousness' sake.

Will you be called "blessed"? When soldiers die on the battlefield, we may call them heroes. When statesmen die for a cause, we may call them patriots. When people die in old age, we may call them venerable. When people die for others, we may call them martyrs. But there is a term that only God can use, a label only he can give: "Blessed"! It is a term or label ascribed to people who are his. The bestowal of that title is not dependent upon our opinion of ourselves; it is God's statement about us.

"Blessed" is not a casual term. It is a special term for a special people, a people obedient to their Savior and Lord and blessed because of it throughout all eternity. And the blessed ones have peace.

God had something so important to say about this blessing that when he gave his message to John he said emphatically, "Write it down." "And I heard a voice from heaven saying unto me, Write, Blessed are the dead which die in the Lord from henceforth: Yea, saith the Spirit, that they may rest from their labours; and their works do follow them" (Revelation 14:13, KJV). Blessed! Happy! The blessed are happy as they live in the Lord and happy when they die in the Lord—they have his inner peace.

The emphasis is on the word "in." We die in the Lord because we have lived in the Lord. For some that is for a blessed lifetime, for others a blessed last breath; for those who refuse him, even to the end of life, it is never. If we are in him, abiding in him, living as new creatures in him, then we will also die in him. "Blessed are they who die in the Lord. They rest from their labors; their works do follow them." Our works don't go ahead of us; they follow. Jesus is ahead of us. God sees Jesus, then us, and our works follow after.

The "blesseds" make all the difference in how we live. Inner peace and stability come to us as a result of being his. I know a man who has been suffering with extreme pain for years. In all this time he has let the "blesseds" in his own life flow out to other people. He is a man at peace because he is a man with the blesseds of God—and he offers what he has.

Watch people when they face death or financial reverses or any critical change. The people who suffer the most are the ones who don't know how to live without their social, financial, or physical crutches. But watch the follower of Jesus. The difference is dramatic; he has peace. He is the blessed one.

Not only is the difference obvious in the physical and the material realm, but in the psychological too. Who would believe that a person can face "reviling and all manner of evil falsely" and not be personally destroyed? But he can, just as Jesus promised in the Beatitudes.

It is painful to be victimized when you are trying to do what is right. It hurts deeply to be criticized, or, even worse, to be persecuted when you are trying to give your best. But the deep peace of Jesus is a blanket of love that covers and soothes the one suffering persecution. The outward happiness may be gone for awhile, but not the deep inner peace and joy.

Following Jesus may seem foolish to those who

don't know him, but when a person can come to the end of his days contented, knowing what it is to be blessed and happy, he will say with certainty that it was the only adventure worth taking.

God's blessing—his peace—is for us. God doesn't leave us comfortless. He knows what he is calling us to and knows why he is calling us to it. He has peace for those who follow him such as no person or situation can provide. Following him is an adventure with blessings. We live in the pleasure of his company.

Pray about your life, every part of it. Present your life to him. See what he will do with it. Join the band of God's friends—the others around you who are following Jesus. It is the "peace-full" life, the blessed life, now and forever. It is the gateway to happiness; not excitement always, or bubbling joy constantly, but happiness—real, deep happiness. So come, be a friend of God. Come, live in the pleasure of his company. Come, live a happy life.

# TWELVE
# Come, Live a Happy Life

† *For I know the thoughts that I think toward you,*
*saith the Lord, thoughts of peace, and not of evil, to*
*give you an expected end. Then shall ye call upon me,*
*and ye shall go and pray unto me, and I will hearken*
*unto you. And ye shall seek me, and find me, when ye*
*shall search for me with all your heart. And I will be*
*found of you, saith the Lord* [Jeremiah 29:11–14, KJV].

God designed me to be happy. Knowing this is not
some form of self-hypnosis or an attempt to convince
myself against all reality. Happiness is not an act that I
perform or a mask that I put on. It is a truth. It is
based on the assurance that God himself holds my
life. It is an awakening to who I am in him. It is
knowing that I don't have to wait to become or have
something; I can start to live fully, totally, obediently
where I am. This is a happy life—now.

"But that's unrealistic."

"You are in the real world."

At least that's what some people say when they listen to an explanation of this happy adventure called
following Jesus Christ. But that's not really a conviction that they hold, it's a wish—a very sad wish. It is
a wish built on a fearful hope that discipleship won't

work, because if it does, and they are not practicing it or experiencing it, they will be unhappy now and forever.

There are always going to be people around who tell us why obedience to the teachings of Jesus isn't realistic, even when deep down inside those same people suspect that obedience to him and his teachings is realistic. Those who speak the loudest against the disciplines of obedience are usually the ones who are most certain deep down inside that theirs would be a different life if they ever did obey him. They want "happiness," but they don't understand what it is. Certainly they can't imagine that it comes from following Jesus. They don't have friendship with God; they aren't disciples. They don't know what this dimension of life is. But we know.

"The disciple is not above his master: but every one that is perfect shall be as his master" (Luke 6:40, KJV). We will be like Jesus.

"Whoever he be of you that forsaketh not all that he hath, he cannot be my disciple" (Luke 14:33, KJV). If we follow him, we may end up poorer than even the foxes who "have holes, and the birds of the air [who] have nests" (Matthew 8:20, KJV), but we will follow him anyway.

Such a life sounds undesirable to pursue and impossible to live, and in our own strength it is. But Jesus calls us to it because he calls us to himself. In him everything else becomes relative. If we have property, it is his, whether we are called to give it up or keep it. Our money is his and our families are his. That's not a frightening thought: if we do what he asks, he takes care of his own.

The one who is surrendered in obedience to Jesus

Christ can relax and live and enjoy himself whether he has much or very little—because logically, sensibly, through good counsel and with prayer, he is doing what he knows God has asked him to do. To those who won't trust God, such an act seems foolish. To those who do trust God, anything else is foolish.

Unrealistic?

Who is going to stand before Jesus Christ and tell him that what he teaches is unrealistic?

Just "holy" talk?

Who is going to go to God the Father and tell him that Jesus is just making noises, strange "holy" word-sounds?

Who is going to tell God that his Son doesn't mean what he says or tell him, "I think you are mistaken," or say, "I looked at what Jesus said, but then I looked at my own logic, and frankly, God, my own logic makes a lot more sense"? Who is going to say those things?

He has given his Word for us to build upon. Ignore that, or substitute our own fragile words for it, and we have crumbling stones or sand. Dietrich Bonhoeffer, who followed Jesus, returned to Hitler's Germany and died for his faithfulness to Christ. Bonhoeffer explained what obedience and faithfulness means: "The word which we fail to do is no rock to build a house on. There can then be no union with Jesus. He has never known us. That is why as soon as the hurricane begins we lose the word, and find that we have never really believed it. The word we had was not Christ's, but a word we had wrested from Him and made our own by reflecting on it instead of doing it. So our house crashes in ruins, because it is not founded on the word of Jesus Christ."

Following Jesus is not a burden. Following church dogma can be a burden. Following certain theological pronouncements can be a burden. Trying to be good can be a burden. Trying to be obedient by our own "logic" can be a burden. But following Jesus is never a burden.

"His commandments are not burdensome" (1 John 5:3, NASB), we are told, and they're not. Where did the idea ever start that they were? It probably started with people who never tried to follow Christ or, worse, tried to follow the Master without first surrendering their lives to him. His commands without his indwelling Spirit cannot be kept.

Following him is not determined by our own feelings about following him. We do not obey *our* concept of his commands. Following him means following what he teaches, being prayerfully aware that Scripture is not to be filtered through our own method of determining what is important for us and what is not.

Following Jesus is not provisional. We do not follow him on our terms, we follow him on his. If there were conditions, those conditions would monopolize our thinking and our time. We are to be monopolized by him. One man who approached Jesus tried to put conditions on his obedience. He said, "Permit me first to go and bury my father" (Matthew 8:21, NASB). Jesus wouldn't accept that.

The man was putting up his own condition. It came between him and Jesus. Anything can become a condition. Even following him for what he may do for me spiritually or emotionally or physically is a condition. I do not follow him because it feels good. I do not follow him because he provides bread or water or escape, but because he asks me to follow him. It must be that way. We sign the bottom of the contract. He fills in the top.

It is a famous saying now, though it was new when Dietrich Bonhoeffer said it: "When Christ calls a man, He bids him come and die."

That's true! We are no longer our own; we are crucified with Christ, yet we are alive because we are born again to new life in him. And the life we once had (though it was in reality no life at all) is gone. We are alive in him because we have already died, and what we have in Christ now is "eternal" life. Everything is changed. The values we had while we were dead are no longer the values we have in our new life in Christ. We have died! One cannot live in Christ until he passes from death into life.

It is interesting that new Christians seem to know that this is true and start their new life building on the Rock. Then, too often, they are turned away after some exposure to the compromising lives of older Christians. New Christians, having the fresh experience of trusting Jesus as Savior and being prepared to trust him as Lord, approach discipleship with the belief: "It is right and it will work, because Jesus taught it." They believe Romans 8:28 and believe that "all" things mean both the negative and the positive, not just the events in life that are pleasing.

But there are senior Christians who become jaded about life, so they compromise and teach compromise (or what they call "realistic Christianity"). They become the sadly troubled ones who, looking back on their lives, wonder, "Could obedience have worked? What if I had stuck to my earlier convictions about taking Jesus at his word? What would have happened;

what would my life have been if I had followed Jesus as he asked me to do? What would it have been like to have been truly a friend of God?"

And at the end of life, preparing to meet him, many Christians carry guilt because the corruptive things of "moth and rust" had more importance to them while God's friendship had little value. There are Christians who late in life become aware that the life "worked out for myself" was not a fulfilling one and wonder what "he might have worked out for me." And they don't know; they can only guess. They never really lived. They have never been truly happy.

The happy life doesn't mean that we are complete, for completion would mean we would no longer strive. Yet we are fulfilled, for all that he is is fulfilling us. In that sense, the redeemed sense, the spiritual sense, we can be complete even now, for we belong to the One who is completeness.

God is complete, and in his completion is himself our fulfillment and happiness. Nothing more needs to be added. Someday all that I have in hope will be mine in fact. But even now all that he gives is mine, mine to the extent that I allow him to fill me. God can make me happy now and someday even happier. He is happiness. He offers the happy life, the perfect life—because he offers himself.

C. S. Lewis, writing in *Mere Christianity,* said of God: "He meant what He said. Those who put themselves in His hands will become perfect, as He is perfect—perfect in love, wisdom, joy, beauty, and immortality. The change will not be completed in this life, for death is an important part of the treatment. How far the change will have gone before death in any particular Christian is uncertain."

But though the degree is uncertain, the fact is not. We can begin to enjoy to the fullest what we have in him now, to indulge ourselves now in who he is and what he gives. We are brought into wholeness in him through his rescuing and his claiming. We know the fact of "Christ in me." We have been made alive through resurrection life, and everything we are and have—growth, expansion, discipline, enjoyment, happiness, holiness—comes from this. None of this can come to the dead who are decaying, but it does come to the living, the alive in Christ. It is all there for the man or woman of God.

Can I be happy? Of course I can, for I have his life and he is the source and essence of happiness. The question for me is not, "Can I?" but "Will I?" Will I allow that happiness to have its full work in me? Having been made by God and redeemed by God, it is impossible for me to say, "But I cannot be like him," for that would be a contradiction. He has made my being in him possible. John Haggai said, "No one but God stills the mind. No one but God steels the spirit. No one but God thrills the soul."

What is this happiness? Can I explain it? Probably not. Can I measure it? No! Can I experience it? Yes! One cannot measure what happiness is any more than he can measure the holiness that produces it. For we would have to stand still to measure, and we cannot do that. We are growing when we have his life. We are not dead anymore. Tomorrow will be richer for me and fuller and deeper than today. Certainly next year, building as it does on this year, will give an even larger dimension of God's fulfillment.

We often look at a child and say, "What a happy child," and we suppose he is. But he can be even happier when he is forty or seventy. Why? Because his capacity for happiness increases with growth and experience. We tend to mistake simplicity for happiness; we think of not knowing as innocence and mistake absence of problems for peace. But real happiness is knowing and understanding and still having genuine happiness with deep peace. That's what God offers.

Then do holiness and happiness go together? Yes, the one comes from the other. The Apostle Paul speaks of putting off the old self which is being corrupted by deceitful desires and putting on the new self created to be like God in true righteousness and holiness (Ephesians 4:22, 23).

Holiness is like putting on a new suit of clothes— not a patched suit but a new suit. Jesus made it clear that we can't put new cloth on old garments; it won't hold. There are no halfway measures with God, not in obedience, discipleship, happiness, or holiness. As F. P. Harton put it, "A moderately good Christian is as unsatisfactory as a moderately good egg." Both are useless.

There are people who are always looking, always trying to get a sensation or a feeling or an experience, trying to add happiness to what is dead and decaying and rotting—and it can't be done. Jesus Christ is life. "I am the way, the truth, and the life: no man cometh unto the Father, but by me" (John 14:6, KJV). Coming into his life, finding his fulfillment, yielding to him, letting him be all that is holy in us—that's the way to happiness.

In *Mere Christianity* C. S. Lewis wrote, "If you decide to make thrills your regular diet and try to prolong them artificially, they will all get weaker and weaker, and fewer and fewer, and you will be a bored, disillusioned old man for the rest of your life. . . . It is much better fun to learn to swim than to go on endlessly [and hopelessly] trying to get back the feeling you had when you first went paddling as a small boy." Living the happy life is like learning to swim—as you make progress you enjoy it more because you see that you are going somewhere.

You can be happy in your mind because you can be holy in your mind. There is peace for anyone whose mind is stayed on him. That's perfect peace. The mind—a mind that is proving what is that good, acceptable, and perfect will of God—can be renewed toward that peace.

Everything takes on a new perspective when we seek to know him and understand him, and think through, on the basis of who he is, the meaning of holiness. It has nothing to do with accomplishment or education or success or financial stability or social relationships or health. Richard Baxter understood that. In 1650 he said, "Take a poor Christian that can scarce speak true English about religion, that hath a weak understanding, a failing memory, a stammering tongue, yet his heart is set on God: he hath chosen him for his portion; his thoughts are on eternity; his desires there, his dwelling there. . . . I had rather die in this man's condition, and have my soul in his soul's case, than in the case of him that hath the most eminent gifts, and is most admired for parts and duty, whose heart is not thus taken up with God."

If my mind is fixed on him, then money, job, prestige, security or the lack of it take on a totally different significance. World affairs, though they be a concern, are seen in a different perspective. Pleasure, self-seeking, and gain are no longer important. Loneliness becomes something that I can handle, whether or not I like it, because God is my source of happiness. He is in my mind, my heart, and my soul, and he will always be there—forever.

Again, it was Richard Baxter who said, "As we paid nothing for God's eternal love and nothing for the Son of his love, and nothing for his Spirit and our grace and faith, and nothing for our pardon, so shall we pay nothing for our eternal Rest. . . . The broken heart that hath known the desert of sin doth understand and feel what I say. What an astonishing thought it will be to think of the unmeasurable difference between our deservings and our receivings; between the state we should have been in and the state we are in. . . . O, how free was all this love, and how free is this enjoyed glory." He gives the fullness of his love that we may receive it and enjoy it forever.

We can be happy not only in our feelings but in our wills, for it is the will that determines our steps toward holiness. Christians are people who have declared "I will" when they determine to follow Christ. By our wills we have gathered up all that we are—our strengths, weaknesses, talents, gifts, shortcomings, emotional difficulties—and surrendered everything to the living Christ. It is an intentional act. To be a Christian is a step of faith, one made by a definite act of the will. When Jesus called those fishermen and that tax collector, they had to will to follow him. He told stories about those like the rich young ruler who would not.

Thomas Kelly in his *Testament of Devotion* wrote, "The crux of religious living lies in the will, not in transient and variable states. Utter dedication of will to God is open to all. . . . Where the will to will God's will is present, there is a child of God. When there are graciously given to us such glimpses of glory as aid us in softening our will, then we may be humbly grateful. But glad willing away of self that the will of God, so far as it can be discerned, may become what we will—that is the basic condition. It is not our will to be happy that makes us happy. It is that we will to be God's person, that we will to be wholly obedient, that we will to seek his completion in us, that brings happiness. Jesus said, "I came down from heaven, not to do mine own will, but the will of him that sent me" (John 6:38, KJV). His friends do the same.

Was Jesus happy? I think he was, not because he did what we call "happy" things but because he knew who he was and did what he was sent to Earth to do. The dedication of the will is not just a matter of being better equipped, better educated, better trained, and having better opportunities; but through the Holy Spirit it is determining to live obediently in the perfect will of God.

Happiness goes with holiness. The soul is the God-breathed part of us that distinguishes a human being from all the rest of creation. We are uniquely and purposely created for holiness, happiness, and peace.

People don't ask it very often of each other, but they should because it is the most important question, the only one with eternal dimensions: "Is it well with your soul?" We need to ask that. It is a reminder of what is important.

We ask, "How are you?" "How is business?" "How is the family?" We even ask, "How is your car running?" We need to be asking, "Is it well with your soul?"

Thomas Kelly said, "The life that intends to be wholly obedient, wholly submissive, wholly listening, is astonishing in its completeness. Its joys are ravishing, its peace profound, its humility the deepest, its power world-shaking, its love enveloping, its simplicity that of a trusting child. It is the life and power in which the prophets and apostles lived. It is the life and power of Jesus of Nazareth, who knew that 'When thine eye is single, thy whole body is full of light' (Luke 11:34, KJV)."

We come into peace and happiness when we give the soul back to him. He alone has right of ownership. Through his redemption the soul is purchased with the price that is higher than any price ever paid for anything—the shed blood of Jesus. The soul comes once more as the prodigal son did—to its proper home—and begins to live "at home" in a secure and expanding life.

The first act of the soul is the act of surrender. But it is not a single act; it is a continuing act. Let it always be that act throughout all of life. For the happy person is the surrendered person, the one who belongs knowingly and intentionally to God.

Because we are not fragmented beings and because we are not just matter or emotion but both and more, the happiness that is ours is a happiness that is central to all that life is. William Law said, "If, therefore, we are to live unto God at any time, or in any place, we are to live unto Him at all times, and in all places. If we are to use any thing as the gift of God, we are to use every thing as His gift. If we are to do any thing by strict rules of reason and piety, we are to do every thing in the same manner. Because reason, and wisdom, and piety, are as much the best things at all times, and in all places, as they are the best things at any time or in any place." And then he added, "He therefore is the devout man, who lives no longer to his own will, or the way and spirit of the world, but to the sole will of God; who considers God in every thing, who serves God in every thing, who makes all the parts of his common life parts of piety, by doing every thing in the Name of God, and under such rules as are conformable to His glory."

You do not function in parts; you are a whole. Your life encompasses all that you are. Every minute is experienced by the "all" of you. Your difficulties cannot be compartmentalized; neither can your joys. If your situation changes in any way, it changes for your whole person. If you face a responsibility or a task or an adventure, you face it not in segments of yourself but with your whole being. If you fall into failure, it is not just the failure of your mind or your will or your body; it is a failure of you.

We live a life that is new every breathing second. Therefore every second is holy—for every second is his. In knowing that, we can realize the larger dimensions of "happy" because we know it is a product of our total life in him.

Happiness is beyond my understanding of what happiness is, just as God is beyond my understanding of who God is. But if I desire to live with God on his terms and in his way to the best of my understanding, I will have God and I will have his happiness. Enter into this holy life and you will enter into the happy life, for he is the Source of both. Don't settle for anything less. Focus on him. Run the race he sets before you. Look toward eternity and go with Christ.

Philip Doddridge had his eyes focused that way. He said, "ETERNITY! ETERNITY! ETERNITY! Carry the view of it about with you, if it be possible, through every hour of waking life; and be fully persuaded that you have no business, no interest in life, that is inconsistent with it: for whatsoever would be injurious in this view, is not your business, is not your interest."

Come, live a holy life. What is there that keeps you from it? Certainly God doesn't keep you from it. He wants that life for you more than you could ever want it for yourself, for he understands all that it will mean to you. He designed you to have it. He redeemed you to have it. He lives for you to have it.

Come, live a happy life.

Come, live a holy, obedient, and disciplined life.

Come, live in the pleasure of his company.

# RESOURCES

Baxter, Richard. *The Saint's Everlasting Rest,* abridged with an introduction by John T. Wilkinson. The Epworth Press, 1962.

Bonhoeffer, Dietrich. *The Cost of Discipleship.* New York: The MacMillan Company, 1948.

Brunner, Emil. *Eternal Hope,* translated by Harold Knight. Philadelphia: Westminster Press, 1954.

Cailliet, Emile. *Journey into Light.* Grand Rapids: Zondervan, 1968.

Doddridge, Philip. *The Rise and Progress of Religion in the Soul.* Philadelphia: Presbyterian Board of Publication, n.d.

Haggai, John. *How to Win over Loneliness.* Nashville: Thomas Nelson, 1979.

Harton, F. P. *The Elements of the Spiritual Life: A Study in Ascetical Theology.* London: Society for Promoting Christian Knowledge, 1950.

Hunt, George Laird. *Rediscovering the Church.* New York: Association Press, 1956.

Law, William. *A Serious Call to a Devout and Holy Life.* London: Society for Promoting Christian Knowledge, 1910.

Lewis, C. S. *Mere Christianity.* New York: The MacMillan Company, 1975.

Lovelace, Richard F. *Dynamics of a Spiritual Life: An Evangelical Theology of Renewal*. Downers Grove, IL: InterVarsity Press, 1979.

McConkey, James H. *The Surrendered Life*. Kalamazoo, MI: Master's Press, Inc., 1977.

McNeile, A. H. *Discipleship*. London: Society for Promoting Christian Knowledge, 1917.

Smith, Malcolm. *Blood Brothers in Christ*. Old Tappan, NJ: Fleming H. Revell, 1975.

Steinberger, G. *In the Footprints of the Lamb,* translated from the Norwegian edition by Berhard Christensen. Minneapolis: Bethany Fellowship, Inc., 1936.

Thompson, Cameron V. *Master Secrets of Prayer*. Lincoln, NB: Good News Broadcasting Association, Inc., 1959.

Tozer, A. W. *The Pursuit of God*. Harrisburg, PA: Christian Publications, 1948.